3 4143 10066 6328

D0188507

ABOUT THE AUTHOR

Debbie Connolly has worked with animals for 27 years in all disciplines: training, boarding, rescue, showing, behaviour and strays. She travels all over the UK treating animals, including pet livestock. She promotes responsible pet ownership and good breeding practices, and runs **www.safepets.co.uk and www.ethicalbreeding.com**.

Best known for the BBC series *Dog Borstal*, she also appeared in *Britain's Most Embarrassing Pets*. She is the feature writer for London Dog forum and has had articles published in everything from the *Veterinary Times* to the *Police Billboard* magazines. She is an Associate Member of the British Institute of Professional Dog Trainers.

BETTER
DOG
BEHAVIOUR

UNDERSTAND THE
DYNAMICS OF
HUMAN/DOG
RELATIONSHIPS

Debbie Connolly

Constable & Robinson Ltd
3 The Lanchesters
162 Fulham Palace Road
London W6 9ER
www.constablerobinson.com

First published by Right Way,
an imprint of Constable & Robinson, 2011

A copy of the British Library Cataloguing in Publication Data
is available from the British Library

ISBN: 978-0-7160-2274-9

Printed in Great Britain by Clays Ltd, St Ives plc

1   3   5   7   9   10   8   6   4   2

DEDICATION

To my Nanna who taught me to read and gave me possibilities.

My love and gratitude to all my friends who have supported the bad and good times and kept me going.

Special thanks and love to Chris and Jen, my lovely family.

CONTENTS

1

IT'S JUST A DOG

Humanizing dog behaviour and imagining that dogs are saying and feeling things they couldn't possibly say or feel are probably the worst and the stupidest things that owners do. Dogs are also often used as emotional weapons between warring family members and have occasionally been the cause of divorces and even violence. Personally I ditched the man and kept the dogs. I always told him there was never any argument about which of them was the most important to me but he didn't listen!

Later chapters will go into more detail about actual training methods, but firstly you need to learn what part humans are playing in causing the problems.

Can dogs feel emotion? My personal feeling is that to some extent they can. They cannot, though, feel guilty, do things on purpose to upset you, exhibit behaviour when you have visitors that is specifically designed to embarrass you, understand a conversation or cook dinner. If they could do these things, we'd be their pets, not the other way round. Here is the best (and worst) example I can think of.

I arrived at a smart Victorian semi and could hear the German Shepherd I had come to sort out barking furiously as

I got out of the car. I knew this dog had bitten badly on at least two occasions, so I was a little apprehensive to say the least. This sort of work is what I specialize in but I'm not Rambo and I wiped my sweaty palms on my coat before knocking. This girl was owned by an elderly couple who I knew spoiled her and I thought I was prepared for the usual lecture about treating her as a dog and not a child. However, I was wrong. It wasn't quite the usual lecture . . .

It took some time for me to get into the house whilst the offending dog was shut into another room and two smiling people greeted me, seemingly oblivious to the murderous noise coming from the kitchen. We sat down and had a long discussion in loud voices whilst the noise abated somewhat. Because this dog was aggressive over food, I had deliberately arranged to be there at dinner time to see them all eating, so in due course we went out into the dining room and the dog was let in. As expected she charged at me barking and I used several swear words to illustrate the fact that I wasn't scared (I was but she didn't need to know). The lady and gentleman went out into the kitchen and for several minutes went through the routine of setting the table, setting three places. The dog watched intently and, as the actual food was carried in, they looked at her and said "chair" firmly and she jumped up onto one of the dining chairs where a place was set and a plate of human food was placed in front of her.

I was so gob smacked I stood for several seconds probably with my mouth gaping open. I then looked around the room suspiciously, convinced there must be hidden cameras and that either Noel Edmonds or Jeremy Beadle was about to jump out at me and that one of my friends would have to be firmly slapped for setting me up. Of course, that wasn't going to happen. These lovely people had lost the plot. This dog was a family member to them and therefore had to sit with them at dinner. The funny thing about this is that they had worked so hard to get this dog not just to sit at the table, but only to get on the chair when told, and only to get down when told. She wasn't allowed to gobble her food, she had to eat steadily and so had table manners that would put most children to shame. In fact, when grandchildren visited, they were told to "Watch Candy and see how to behave."

The effect this treatment had on the dog was catastrophic. German Shepherds are a strong willed, dominant breed with guarding and territorial tendencies. They are a breed that can see gaps in leadership and fill them quite effectively. Dogs do not see unlimited love as kindness, they see it as weakness. Love alone will not train a dog nor gain its respect. Without rules and boundaries most dogs will develop some sort of problem. This dog adored her owners and they adored her even more, but she had no respect for them and this meant none for anyone else.

The dining table behaviour was the tip of the iceberg. When she had bitten the last time, they had sat the dog down and explained to her how upset they were and how disappointed they were with her. They claimed she understood this and looked sorrowfully at the floor, embarrassed. All the time they were telling me this, Candy was glaring at me with a definite homicidal look in her eyes. Every time one of the owners looked directly at her, her expression softened and she smiled at them, then went back to glaring at me. Clever girl she was. Trying to explain to these people that the dog was not embarrassed or upset was impossible. The dog was reacting to their body language and simply trying to appease their annoyance without any idea of what they were talking about. I hadn't got very far into telling them what had to change before they both started to cry. I'd only just got to the "She can't eat human food and sit at the table" before tears welled up and they both dabbed at their eyes with hand-kerchiefs.

So what could I do? This was much harder to deal with than all the owners who argue and talk rubbish about how they have "tried everything". I can shout at them and point out the error of their ways. This was completely different; I had no idea how to tackle them. When I said she couldn't sleep with them any more and had to be left downstairs, a fresh flood of tears started and they said, "We can't do that to her, she will become suicidal and hate us." The sad thing is that they meant it. They really believed that this dog's feelings would be so injured she would never speak to them again. So I thought I was really clever in trying a new tactic. I told them she was very stressed by the pressure they put on her to constantly be in charge and guarding them. I said that she must be quite upset at being given so much responsibility and that was why she was over-reacting and biting people. Their faces gradually changed and they started looking guilty and concerned. Great, I had cracked it. I went on about how they should take more responsibility by telling her what to do more and give her time off from guarding by having her sleep downstairs and stay in a room alone for short periods. They started nodding in agreement and I thought for one day that was enough for them to digest and I got up to leave, feeling rather clever. I handed to them the notes I had made and said I would come back in a week and see how it was going. We got to the door and I reached to shake hands and the dog promptly bit me on the hand. My fault really, but the lady grabbed the dog and started stroking her furiously, saying, "Don't worry, she's going. We won't do any of those horrible things to you that she said." The man

Rules and boundaries

• Always teach your dog basic obedience, without it you have nothing.

• If you give a command, follow it through and get a result.

• Make sure that the person who gives the command is the one who enforces it; everyone else is to mind their own business.

• Don't allow the dog privileges it can misinterpret as you giving it power; this means height the same as or higher than you, food sharing, access to territory.

• Your dog cannot ever feel human emotions. Don't allow bad behaviour because you think the dog is upset, or will hate you for shouting, or was woken suddenly.

• Be consistent. Everyone in the family should have the same standards and commands.

• Don't be flattered by a dog that "guards" you by growling at people who approach you or by barking at people and dogs in the street. This is not guarding; it is "claiming" you.

seemed a little embarrassed as he looked at the blood on my hand and said, "We'll calm her down and give her one of her special biscuits. She'll be fine soon," and shut the door. I never did find out if he meant the biscuit was for the dog or his wife.

What was the outcome of this story? Sadly the dog was put to sleep about six months later. The owners never could change their management and relationship with the dog and she escaped one day and attacked the first person she met and had to be put down. A terrible waste of a very clever dog.

Owners can be really offended by their dog's behaviour. They say things like, "My dog is so ungrateful," and "After the good home I've given this dog I can't believe how it behaves." No dog can ever be grateful for what you do. Dogs can enjoy their lives with you and have a pleasant and loving environment to live in, but that won't make them behave properly. Only training and sensible rules will do that. Would you allow your children to walk away instead of doing what you asked? Would you allow them to pull at your clothes and shout at you to get your attention when on the phone or stopping to speak to someone? Would you allow them to sit drooling near you whilst you eat your dinner? Would you allow them to bite your visitors (anyone who says it depends on the visitor is in trouble)? No! Then why let your dog do it?

I am often given examples of dogs supposedly showing real feelings. These stories often take the form of a dog that seems sad when the owner is sad and the owner feels that the dog is showing empathy. Also owners tell me about dogs that show distress and upset if another pet in the household has died. It would be nice to think that dogs had these sorts of feelings and therefore could feel these things for us. However, it is also likely that the loss of a pack member is a traumatic experience that threatens your dog's own security. Most dogs react to a sad person by looking concerned and submissive. It is a safety tactic as they can't understand what is wrong or how to make things OK again. I'd like to believe it too; there are things my own dogs and cats have done that I'd love to interpret as emotion but I'll never prove it was true!

Another common problem I see is when dogs are used as

pawns in relationships. The dog often becomes the scape-goat for the bad feelings one human feels for another. It is not uncommon for couples to mentally retire to their corners with one of them defending the dog to death, while the other picks on every little thing it does. This is often a result of one person doting too much on the dog to the detriment and sometimes exclusion of the other person or feelings of jealousy on one side.

I once went to see an older couple with two Jack Russell Terriers, a dog and a bitch. The bitch had been with them a while and the dog was about 18 months old and had come from a rescue centre about three months earlier. The bitch was fine, a little yappy, but that's terriers. The dog though was a bossy little thing that showed his teeth whenever the lady tried to tell him to do anything and had now started to bite her even if she was trying to stroke him. The dog adored the man and sat quite happily with him and let him do anything. It was obvious when I arrived that the lady wore the trousers in this house. She was a formidable person, with a booming voice and a very assertive person-ality. She even gave orders to her husband as if commanding a dog. The husband was a nice, gentle soul who seemed rather hen-pecked.

The consultation was made difficult by the fact that the lady kept answering all the questions, even when I asked the man.

"So what good points does this dog have?" I asked, optimistically as she just seemed to want to tell me how horrible it was.

"Well he's a good looking Jack but not very bright," she said.

I wondered if she used the same criteria for picking men.

All the time we were talking, the man kept putting his head down slightly and petting the dog. It was a bit odd and so I watched to see exactly when he was doing it. It seemed that whenever we were specifically talking about the dog being aggressive and biting her, his head dropped. When she commented on how horrible the dog was and how he would have to go if he didn't stop biting her and ended all her sentences with "Isn't that right dear?" he did it again and didn't actually answer.

It dawned on me that the reason he kept looking down was because he was hiding a laugh or at least a smirk. He also couldn't bring himself actually to say that the dog was bad or naughty. This made me smirk too as I guessed the reason why he felt like this.

I asked the lady to make some coffee knowing in their old house that the kitchen was a long way back. Once she had gone, I didn't have time to mess about, so I turned to the man.

"Do you admire this dog?" I asked. He stared at me and went a bit pink.

"Erm . . . I don't know what you mean, what could I admire him for?"

"For doing what you daren't do, answering back," I said firmly.

"Oh God, is it obvious?"

"Am I right then, do you wish you had the courage this dog has?"

He laughed loudly and nodded his head.

"I wish I had his balls," he whispered, patting the dog firmly on the head.

His wife came back and we both had to suppress giggles. I too had a sneaking admiration for the dog but he really had to be stopped. To be fair to the husband, he did play his part in the treatment. A lot of the dog's aggression stemmed from the fact that he petted the dog even when it was being a pain. If the wife told the dog off, it would run to him and get a fuss and then often charge back at her to bite her. Once this stopped and he started to give commands to the dog and only praise him when he instigated it and minded his own business when his wife was dealing with the dog, it all stopped.

It isn't just the actual owners who use dogs to prove points either. Once when training a very food aggressive and generally aggressive Labrador I allowed the mother-in-law to come to the final training session. This lady looked after the dog three days a week whilst the people went to work and thoroughly spoiled him. The dog was owned by a sensible professional couple in their late thirties who took on board everything I said and were a joy to work with. However, the mother-in-law was mentioned frequently as they both felt she wouldn't follow the new regime and they couldn't risk this dog biting again as the police had already been involved.

We arranged for her to be present for the final session in the hope that as an outsider she would take it from me as she didn't listen to them. Her biggest crime was allowing the dog to sit next to her on the sofa whilst she hand fed him cat biscuits. He had been sitting next to a neighbour's child and had bitten her when she didn't have any biscuits for him but even this had not stopped this rather obnoxious woman from doing something so stupid. So I knew I had my work cut out.

The owners sat opposite me at my desk and the mother-in-law (it was the wife's mother) sat towards the back of the office against the wall. She had a handbag perched firmly on her lap which the dog kept sniffing enthusiastically. No prizes for guessing what she had in there. I launched into my full lecture to cover all the training points regarding how the changes had been achieved and what the future plan was. Every time I said anything about stopping this dog from getting on furniture or sitting on people, or anything to do with him not staring or drooling over people when they were eating, I got the same reaction. Mother-in-law would stare at me and roll her eyes.

I am not the most patient of people and after about 20 minutes I had had enough of her. I put down my pen and addressed her in my best dog training voice.

"What exactly is the matter with you?" I asked, staring at her for a change. She looked a little startled.

"What do you mean?"

"Don't waste my time. You have been sitting rolling your eyes for 20 minutes. Either say what you have to say or get out of my office. These people have spent time and money trying to save this dog's life and you are being an idiot. Now what do you want to say?"

The effect on the couple was more dramatic than on her. The husband nearly spat his coffee onto the desk and his wife just froze and stared at her shoes. Finally, a shocked mother-in-law spoke.

"I can't see how not letting him have a cuddle or have a few treats will stop him biting," she sneered.

"Then you must be deaf or stupid because I have been explaining why for 20 minutes. Not only that, but as you have seen since you got here, he doesn't now show any of the aggressive behaviour he used to. So obviously it works. Why won't you do what you are told?"

She then got braver and argued the points again and got another dressing down from me. It was obvious their fears were justified and she had no intention of changing. The wife was getting a little upset and it was time to draw a halt to this. I used my favourite question to shut her up once and for all. I told her that I would ask her one question and that if she could answer it properly she could do what she liked. I got the owners to turn their chairs to her so they could look at each other and then I asked her the question.

"When you carry on doing everything wrong and the dog carries on biting and gets put to sleep, you will have killed it. So what exactly are you going to say to your daughter and her husband to justify killing their dog?"

Of course, there is no answer. Mother-in-law actually went beetroot and neither her daughter nor her son-in-law could look at her. She grasped her bag and looked a bit upset.

"Right, now either join in, shut up, leave or help. It's up to you," I said calmly and we turned the chairs back round.

For about ten minutes she sat in silence and then gradually said a few things. By the time the session was finished she had chilled out and had even told the dog "no" when he again sniffed at the bag. However, just as I was gathering notes and they were about to leave, the mother-in-law made a comment which then made perfect sense of why she did what she did. The owners were saying how they still wanted to call the dog their baby but they wouldn't treat him like one. This made the mother-in-law look up sharply.

"Of course," she said slowly and deliberately, "I don't actually have any *grandchildren*."

So there it was. The whole thing was her way of trying to make them feel guilty about the fact she had no grandchildren to spoil and had to make do with a dog. Without this weapon to beat them with, she felt she had no way of getting at them and that was why she didn't want to stop. I think I'll take up human psychology next; I'm gradually getting the experience.

Q&A

Is it OK if just one person takes all the responsibility for feeding, grooming and exercising?

No! Some dogs can decide that one person is the boss and nobody else has any power. This can cause aggression and a badly behaved dog as some people give orders and have rules, and some don't. This can be stressful for a dog.

My husband gets a better response from the dog than me. It listens to him more, what can I do?

I hear this comment all the time. Nine times out of ten it isn't true. Men have harsher body language, deeper voices and usually shout more readily than women. That is what the dog is responding to. If neither person can get the dog to respond to a command given in a normal tone of voice, then neither has control or respect. Screaming at a dog to get it to obey is NOT training or control.

My dog hates me. It chews things up when I go out, barks at me, messes on the floor on purpose to upset me and licks its genitals in front of visitors. Why doesn't it like me?

Utter garbage. You have a dog that has no manners, training or respect. I bet you have never been to any training classes and I bet you don't walk the dog or play with it enough. I expect you play fight and play tug-of-war with this dog and it has learned to challenge you and bite you and now you are paying the price. Join a training class.

I like to dress my dog in clothes. Is this a problem?

Personally I think people who do this are trying to fulfil a psychological need. However, the principle of a dog allowing itself to be pushed and pulled and handled is a good one, although if I saw a dog in clothes I would have to come and remove them. And, yes, that applies to bandanas too.

2

MY OTHER DOG IS A ROTTWEILER

I wonder sometimes why people have particular dogs. Some men won't have small dogs. They feel it is a reflection on their macho pride if they are seen walking a Poodle down the street. Owners often have dogs that, whether they realize it or not, are reflections of themselves. One couple arrived with a Mastiff who was a nasty piece of work.

"What made you buy that slavering lunatic?" I asked using my best technical terms.

"I didn't, I married him," she smiled.

It is not uncommon to have couples come to me for consultations where they have a large dog and the dog was the husband's choice and the wife didn't want a big dog. I know it's generalizing, but a lot of men pick large dogs that get left at home with their wife and they go off to work all day and don't have to deal with it. Men also are keen on having large dogs with an edge of aggression to them. Sometimes when I am trying to retrain a dog that bites, a man will show a little reluctance to get rid of the behaviour totally. After one long day with an idiot man with his

Doberman who was a lovely dog but lunged at anything and everything and whose owner wanted the dog to continue to threaten to bite but stop when he said, I simply looked him in the eye and said: "Just how small *is* your penis?"

OK I'm blaming men for everything and it isn't true that they are always at fault. Just often. It tends to be men who play fight with dogs, encouraging tug-of-war games and the like. These are NOT games to a dog, they are challenges. Why would you teach an animal with a large set of sharp teeth to grab you and pull things from you? However, some people think they are proving something and flatter themselves that they always win and so are totally in control. Utter rubbish. Dogs do not say to each other, "Hey, try and take this off me." They actually say "You can't have it, it's mine."

I run a rescue centre that specializes in German Shepherd Dogs so I see a lot of dogs with working potential. I am lucky enough to have good relationships with several police forces who take these dogs and I go on training days with them. Dogs with reluctant bites are played with in exactly this type of way: pulling and dragging things, grabbing and wrestling people. It is a way of encouraging a confident, bold bite from a dog, NOT a game and it doesn't matter if you think you can win every time.

The nicest of dogs and breeds can be ruined by the wrong sort of play. I saw a Labrador bitch that was from working stock and was a clever dog that learned quickly. She was about two when I met her, a family pet with two young children. The husband was in the forces and had been constantly play fighting with this dog and even encouraged his mates to do it. Of course, this dog was maturing and was putting real pressure into it and had started being very aggressive to visitors and even the children. The police had been called when the husband was on his way back from a walk with the dog and a neighbour stopped to say hello as they reached home and the dog flew at her, biting her arm and puncturing it. Finally he agreed they needed help.

It took a long time to convince this idiot that it was his behaviour that had made the dog aggressive; there was nothing actually wrong with the dog. Tensions were very strained between the couple. She was furious as she had been telling him this forever and he wouldn't listen. It was obvious that his priority was looking hard in front of his mates. He made several comments like, "They'll think I've gone soft and can't control my dog." I asked him what was more important: keeping the dog alive and his kids safe or his image? Was looking hard more important than protecting his kids?

By the end of the session he was talking more sensibly but I wasn't convinced. I kept the dog with me for a week whilst I sorted out her problems and they took a work pack home to do some homework with. The dog was brilliant. Clever, easy to train, funny and very affectionate. When they came back a week later, the dog had been transformed. She ran happily to greet them, didn't jump up, didn't grab, let the kids groom her. They were thrilled – all except the husband. He said the dog had "gone soft". About three weeks later I got a call from the wife. The dog was growling again and had snapped at one of the children. I asked her if she thought her husband was still play fighting with the dog. She said when she was there he wasn't, but she had noticed that the dog was jumping up at him again. I went out to see them and used a simple test to see if he had done it again. Remember that I had trained this dog not to react to specific arm movements. Of course, the dog grabbed me and I went mad. He still insisted he wasn't doing it but his wife said she had spoken to his mates and that they said after a few drinks they would come back and play rough with the dog.

A huge row blew up between them and I took the dog back with me for a few days. When they collected her he was very contrite and he agreed he would stop. One of the things he would do to wind the dog up was to clap over her head. This proved to be very significant.

About four weeks later the lady rang me and was in tears. She said her husband had continued to show off with his mates and that the dog was again aggressive. That morning the dog had been lying in front of a small bookcase and one of the children had been on tiptoes leaning over the dog to get a piece of paper from the top of it. The paper had fallen off and fluttered down and, of course, the child had grabbed it by clapping her hands together under and over it. The dog saw this and came straight up off the floor and grabbed the girl's arm, ripping it open. She said she knew that the dog should be put down but she didn't want to do it. I could hear her husband in the background shouting, blaming the dog, saying he was going to kill it.

I told her I didn't think the dog deserved to be dead, but I'd happily euthanize her husband. I told her to give me the dog and I would again retrain it but it would be rehomed. The little girl, bless her, still loved the dog and, although she has a small scar, it wasn't as bad as it might have been. So the dog came to me and three weeks later the wife turned up and said she wanted the dog back as she had left her husband and was going to divorce him.

"Good choice," I said as I hugged her.

Dog lived happily ever after.

Get the Right Dog

- Don't buy a dog because you saw one in the park or a book and thought it was lovely. You don't live with a picture of a dog; you live with the *actual* dog.

- Do your research. Visit breeders and dog shows so you can see several examples of temperament and ages and behaviour.

- Don't buy a big dog from a working or guarding type if you have no experience or if you have no intention of doing any training.

- What you look like walking it is the least of your worries. What you look like with stitches and bandages or on your police mug shot should be your priority.

- Don't buy a working breed version of a popular breed unless you can train a dog properly. A dog bred to be stimulated and occupied eight hours a day is not going to sit on your rug quietly whilst you go to work.

- Don't get *any* dog if you have no intention of going to training classes or putting in any effort. Most of the dogs in rescue are victims of lazy owners who never taught their dogs manners or commands and then ditched them when they got on their nerves.

I know people who go through several dogs in a short space of time. There is a family that bought a Labrador puppy and proudly showed it off to the neighbours. The poor dog was dragged around the garden by the kids, round the street by them and never went to a single lesson or was taken anywhere by the adults. When it reached about seven months old it was very aggressive, pulled badly on the lead, threw itself six feet through the air at visitors and barked continuously. One day it disappeared. About four weeks later the family got a Cocker Spaniel puppy. Same story . . . kids ruined it, it never got any training and at five months it bit one of them badly and it too disappeared. Next they got a Boxer puppy that lasted until 12 months old, but only because they greedily bred a litter from her. She was too young, had no health tests and she too disappeared.

They came to my rescue kennels having decided that they had been really "unlucky" in finding so many badly bred dogs and couldn't believe how hard it was to find a "good dog". I told them that there was only one dog that I thought was suitable for them and I would go and fetch it. They smiled happily until I came back with a stuffed toy dog my friend had bought me.

"This one is perfect. You can be as lazy and selfish as you like and always blame it and yet it will never be naughty." They left.

Some people just never learn from their mistakes. I was asked to train a Boxer who was a five-year-old male. He had been in his current home for nearly three years. Over the Christmas period he had bitten his owner badly on the hand when he took his collar to put him in another room when a visitor arrived. Just before New Year he had bitten the wife's mother badly on the hand too when she leaned over him to put something on the Christmas tree. They had asked a rescue centre to take him but the people there were not sure about rehoming a biting dog so they asked me to see if I could do something with him.

Captain was a large brindle and white male who was very stroppy. He stood on you, pushed you aside to get somewhere and basically just did as he pleased. He knew a few commands but had never been made to do them. I had some information from the owners but I was sure I hadn't been given the full story. During an assessment it transpired he was very food aggressive and would not be restrained or groomed under any circumstances and he would bite as a first resort. Although they denied any other aggression at first, he also turned out to be aggressive with visitors, terrible with other dogs and wanted to kill them and would never get off furniture.

So this was a much bigger problem than they had first confessed to. They got a huge telling off from me as this dog was more dangerous than they admitted to and was a risk to me and my staff. Fair enough if they told me and I agreed, but they hadn't.

Captain was trained by me for nearly four weeks. He turned out to be a clever Boxer and his obedience would put some German Shepherds to shame! He was hard work and bit me twice but we got there in the end. Finally, they were booked to come and get him and do their own training. They didn't get to see Captain until after two hours' lecturing from me. Eventually they came to the training area and were thrilled at this chilled out, well behaved lad that was still every bit a clownish Boxer.

We spent some time discussing dominance and what it was all about. They had always gone round any problems with him rather than solving them. The first issue had been that he bit them when they tried to get him off the sofa soon after getting him. Instead of sorting it out, they simply decided not to get him off any more and this was their basic tactic for any problem. So Captain decided he was in charge and the list of things he didn't want to do grew and grew. He finally decided he wouldn't do anything at all and wouldn't let people touch him or stand over him and that's where my involvement had become inevitable.

As we talked, they told me about their three previous Boxers.

"We've been unlucky," the lady said, "All the Boxers we had before were dominant too. They were all aggressive like him."

Dear God, they still hadn't got the point after five hours of training. It was their management and behaviour that made all the dogs aggressive and dominant.

"All your future dogs are unlucky too. They are all going to bite people and be dead prematurely," I hissed. "Have you really missed the point so badly?"

They were rather shocked and I went through it all again, a little less politely. I am pleased to say that they eventually did understand and several months later my dog won a "best behaved dog" award at a dog show!

It isn't always stupid behaviour that creates a problem with a dog. It can be a mistake made with the best of intentions. I met a lovely lady in her sixties who had a Labrador bitch of about three years old. Her husband had died about 12 months earlier and the dog had been a gift from her to him; they both knew he was dying and this was a long wanted dog.

On his deathbed he had asked her to take care of Honey, the dog, and she had understandably promised she would. When her husband died, the dog was the only tangible link with her husband and Honey became her emotional crutch. The dog went from a fairly disciplined life to one of simply following her mistress around and doing what she liked. Unfortunately, this meant she gradually became harder and harder to handle and her owner felt it was grief and so offered even less discipline. Honey slept with her Mum, sat for hours whilst they cried over their loss and they went everywhere together.

Unfortunately, this made Honey a spoilt brat and she became very aggressive within a few months. Scared of also losing the dog on top of her husband, the lady had hidden the problem and got more and more upset about it. Once I explained that the dog was happier with boundaries and that her husband was not in heaven watching her and thinking she was cruel and that we could solve the problem, she sobbed her heart out. When the rules were back in place, Honey became the good dog she always had been.

It would help if people actually did some research about the dog they buy before buying it. One woman rang me complaining about the Border Collie she had bought. It was about eight months old and bought via a newspaper advert. She said that ever since she got it, it kept running round the kids, gathering up toys and circling them and nipping the back wheels of her pushchair. Of course, this was all normal collie behaviour as I pointed out; the dog was simply mimicking how it would herd sheep.

She laughed disdainfully.

"I didn't get it from a *farm* you idiot," she said laughing. I put the phone down . . .

I have read that children can pick up fears of things like spiders from their parents or from other role models; we are not born with these fears. Dogs too seem capable of picking up their owners' fears. I have seen dogs that shake almost on command and hide from loud noises and from other dogs and even once from ducks! All of these were fears transmitted by the owner's own fear; it was a learned response. Be careful that you are not seeing your own behaviour mirrored in your dog; it isn't pleasant!

If you are a person who is loud, belligerent, impatient

and pushy, you are likely to end up with a dog just the same or one that is highly strung and fearful. If you are a person who is quiet, submissive, gentle and soft, you will get a dog that is calm and steady or one that bullies you. Choose the right dog to fit who you are, not the prettiest one in a book.

Q&A

I have had dogs all my life so surely I don't have to go to classes with the next one, I can train it myself?

No, you can't. I hate that expression, "I've had dogs all my life." Just how many dogs can people have in one lifetime? Four, maybe five? Since when did that make you an expert? I've had people who have had just two previous dogs and were so big headed they decided they could train any dog and made a mess of it. Besides that, dogs need socializing and every dog is different and responds differently. Only proper training will give the right result.

I grew up with [name of breed here] so I know how to handle one, I'd like to adopt/buy one.

This is more annoying than the first question. Usually the person saying this is about 25, in a relationship and getting her first dog of her own. Whilst it helps to have been brought up with dogs and know what dogs do and have basic respect, it is a million miles away from being the one who has to pay for all the furniture the dog eats. Finding the time to train, walk, feed and play with the dog when the buck stops with you comes as a shock to most people with their first dog. Large strong-minded breeds do not make good first dogs and just because you think you know a breed does not mean your partner does.

Because I work I thought I would get a Labrador/Spaniel/ mongrel as they don't need any training.

Bet you don't believe people actually say this? They do. Hundreds of Labs go through rescue and most are out-of-control youngsters. There is no dog in the universe that doesn't need training. Even a nice, good-natured, quiet, calm little dog still needs to know what to do when you need to tell it to do something.

I want a guard dog that can defend my property but will be OK with my kids. What should I get?

Get a tape recording of a barking dog and don't get a real dog. There are actually laws about "guard" dogs and they must have a handler present at all times. Usually people mean a dog that barks like the Hound of the Baskervilles when it hears someone and then turns into a pussy cat when you open the door. They also seem to think that the dog should distinguish, probably by telepathic means, which people to actually bite. This is impossible. If you get a dog of a guarding breed, it is likely to bark at noises and intruders. You do NOT need to wind it up to make it do this. This ridiculous behaviour is responsible for dogs being destroyed needlessly. One minute you are saying, "Go on, get them," then you say, "Why did you bite them?" A properly trained dog is a joy and is not dangerous; a wound up family pet is extremely dangerous. I trained a GSD that an idiot woman had been constantly taking to the front door and really making the dog go mad. Several weeks later when a friend arrived, the dog went straight out of the door and badly injured her. The dog was just doing what it had been taught. The owner beat the dog and you can make up your own version of what I said to her and add expletives as necessary.

3

BUYING A DOG

The reason I see most people is because they have obtained a dog badly. Hopefully anyone reading this book will pass on to others the following information and stop people from repeating mistakes that cause misery for dogs and owners alike.

In the first place, the whole family must want the dog. I turn people away if everyone won't come to choose the dog, or one of them stares out of the window saying, "It's his/her dog, nothing to do with me." I don't let dogs go as surprises either, or as gifts for other people.

Once you have a dog, your life becomes restricted. If you have kids of school age, or even no kids, then suddenly you have a responsibility for something that can't be left all day and those after-work drinks become impossible. Kennelling, vets' fees, food and toys all cost money and I know dozens of owners who have had to cancel holidays because the dog was ill at the last minute or they left booking kennels so late there was no space. If you have a lovely home that you have spent money on, that is always clean, with expensive furnishings, can you really cope with the mess a dog makes?

I get calls from people with long-coated dogs who ask

how soon they can clip the hair off? This is because they can't stand hairs all over or are too lazy to brush them. I tell them to take the dog back to where it came from and get something else. Except most dogs shed, even the short-haired ones and the ones that don't still put dirty marks and footprints all over everything.

A girl I once worked with was very unhappy after she got married (I know that's understandable, I would be too). She said she felt that married life was just cleaning up all day. Obviously before marriage she had never cleaned her mother's house! She said that's all she did, all day and it was a huge shock to find out how much cleaning a house needed even with just two people in it.

About 18 months later (yes, she was still married) she came to work and said she had decided to get a dog. I laughed so loudly most of the office looked round. I'd like to tell you I stifled it into an unconvincing cough, but that would be a lie.

"Please don't do it," I begged, "You couldn't clean up after just you and your husband, what the hell do you think it's going to be like with a dog?"

Of course, nobody ever listens and she ended up with a Doberman bitch puppy. It did the usual puppy things, messed everywhere and threw up on carefully chosen furnishings. It ate the furniture and shoes and an expensive leather jacket it found hanging on the stair post (should have hung it up properly). I know you've already guessed the outcome . . . I rescued it and found it a good home. I sincerely hope they never get a dog again.

I have broken this chapter down into separate advice to cover the most common ways people get dogs. Remember that if you don't see it for yourself, it isn't true.

There is a secret language used by people getting rid of dogs. It is similar to estate agent speak where agents describe a garden too small to swing a cat in as "compact".

It is important you can do the translation, so here's some help: first the lie, then the truth:

We are moving house and can't take the dog with us.
We are moving house and not telling the dog.

Someone is allergic.
Nobody is allergic but my son can do a really convincing sneeze.

I have had to go back to work full time and the dog isn't happy.
I have had to go to work full time to pay for all the damage the dog has done. The dog is now very happy as it has more time to do the damage.

My other dog is jealous of this one.
My other dog is a nervous wreck as this dog is insane.

My partner has left me and I can't afford to keep the dog.
My partner has left me because of the dog and he is coming back as soon as I get rid of it.

It's a great guard dog.
This is probably true so if you run a prison or really hate your family and friends, go for it.

It doesn't bite.
It doesn't bite apart from on weekdays and weekends and when it is asleep.

It never barks.
Apart from on weekdays and weekends . . . you know the rest. Get the idea?

Private Buying

This means all those adverts in the papers and all those "friends of friends" who are parting with a dog. Everyone assumes that if someone is rehoming their own dog they will be honest and can be trusted not to give or sell you a dog that may bite you or hurt your children. Think again. It happens all the time.

I got involved in rescuing a Jack Russell Terrier from a young couple. They had seen a newspaper ad for someone offering a Jack free to a good home. They went to see it, taking their two-year-old son with them and it turned out that the people selling were an elderly couple. They said they were going into sheltered housing and dogs weren't allowed. They seemed like the perfect grandparents, tea in china cups, a lolly for the little boy.

The dog seemed fine and the owner was so upset the couple gave her £20 even though the dog was free. The dog went home with them. A couple of hours later they were all in the garden playing with the dog. The husband was throwing a ball and the dog brought it back a few times. At one point the dog dropped the ball near the man's feet and he bent to pick it up. The dog flew at his face, ripping his cheek open.

As you can imagine, all hell was let loose. The child was dragged indoors and the man had to go to hospital. The lady rang the elderly couple immediately and spoke to the old man. He was quiet for a moment and then said:

"The little b****** does it all the time. Go get it put down," and cut her off.

Just shows you, don't trust anybody. Can you believe a seemingly nice old couple let that dog go to a home with a young child and even took £20 for it?

Test everything.

Do what I do if I am asked to rescue a dog and I want to see if what I am being told is true:

- Ask the owners to groom the dog in front of you. If they have kids, get them to do it too.

- Get the owners and kids to take a chew or bone from the dog. Not just toys, food too.

- Watch where the dog is when you arrive. If it has been shut in another room, go out and come back again when it is in the hallway.

- Go into the garden and throw toys for it.

- Make sure you go for a walk with the dog and pass traffic, dogs and people. If the owners tell you that the dog is safe off lead, make them show you.

You might be surprised how many times just asking for these things gets a different response from the one you were expecting. They might be happy to tell a lie to get rid of the dog, but they are not likely to want to get bitten to prove a point.

If someone tells you that the dog is vaccinated, get the card. Vets will give a duplicate if it is lost, so don't fall for the "We've just moved and can't find it" lie. If you are told they have pedigree papers for the dog, see them. Check for tattoos and microchip certificates. You could easily buy a stolen dog.

Breeders

I know quite a few breeders very well in several breeds. There are some I wouldn't buy a dog from. If I was buying a pedigree breed I would not buy one without it being

Kennel Club registered, with the certificate to prove this had happened. The certificate says that the dog is a pure bred dog and that the parents are who the breeder says they are. Nothing, however, is a guarantee. Puppy farm dogs have been sold with KC registrations and people do get prosecuted and banned because they have falsified the registrations. The Kennel Club is the only organization with a proper database where you cannot make up dogs' names and get certificates printed. This is the case with another database, popular with and created by puppy farmers. This database has produced pedigrees and certificates with made-up names, dogs from different breeds on the pedigree and dogs actually dead when the relevant puppy was born. You can put what you like and they print it. The Kennel Club is the only organization which records health test results and automatically puts them on the registrations. So you can see if the puppy's parents were hip scored, or eye tested, etc. Their database goes back generations and if you say a dog was the parent of your litter, the rest is already on the database so you can't change the ancestry.

It is a common con to be told you can have the puppy for, say, £300 without the KC registration or £400 with it, or some sort of ridiculous added on figure. It actually costs £15 to register a puppy, so people telling you this have something to hide. Trading Standards Departments deal with many hundreds of these cases now.

So you need to ask why a pure bred puppy isn't registered and don't fall for the lies.

A puppy isn't registered because of one or more reasons:

• One or both of the parents isn't registered which means the puppy can't be. This increases your chances of paying for a pedigree and getting a mongrel.

- One or both of the parents has been stolen and therefore the "breeder" has no paperwork. This happens far more than you think and is the reason for some dog thefts.

- The original breeder of one or both parents endorsed the Kennel Club registration. A breeder can put endorsements on registrations such as "progeny not eligible for registration". This means any puppies bred from the dog cannot be KC registered. This is done to protect breed lines and can be lifted at the breeder's discretion, usually on condition the dog passes the health tests relevant to the breed. So your puppy could be from parents not health tested and be carrying serious health problems.

- Some people, with maybe just one dog, say they are just breeding "pets" and that only show dogs need the certificates and so they don't have them. This is rubbish. A KC certificate means that the breeder is confirming that this is a pure bred dog. It gives you the information to sue if necessary and to ensure that the parents were health tested before breeding. It is not a requirement of the show ring to have satisfactory health. Genuine breeders health test to improve their breed, not line their pockets.

- Breeders may want to hide the number of litters their dog has produced to fit in with Kennel Club rules. It has become common for unscrupulous breeders to register one litter with the KC and the alternate one with the "other" registration club.

If you are buying, see the parents' and puppies' certificates when you view and the health results. It is not uncommon for a breeder to use a stud dog from another breeder so sometimes only copies of the father's details are available.

These should be freely seen by you and you should go and meet the stud dog. Most owners don't bother and pay the price later when they discover that the dog is not sound in temperament and their puppy is just the same.

Don't buy a puppy if the conditions are dirty or suspicious in any way. Don't buy a puppy if either or both of the parents are hidden from you and you cannot have them in the same room as you and handle them. Most of my clients who have dogs with serious problems bought them in this way.

It is hard to walk away but if you don't you are helping them to make money and encouraging them to breed again. Don't flatter yourself that you are "saving" a puppy; you are just making space for the next one.

Rescue Kennels
Most members of the public think that rescue centres exist only because the people running them genuinely want to save dogs. This is sometimes not true. I know people with rescues who see it as a money-making venture and operate like a supermarket. Some even make you sign forms to say you understand they won't take the dog back no matter what happens. I always say that the easier it is to get a dog from a specific rescue, the worse it is as a rescue. So don't assume when you see the word "rescue" you are dealing with a reputable, helpful organization.

There are different types of rescue:

• Breed rescue clubs. These are often initially set up by breeders to help their own breed. If you want a specific type of dog, this is the best place to start. However, some of them operate like bad dating agencies, simply matching up phone numbers of buyers and sellers, and they never meet the dogs.

- Rescue kennels. These are sometimes charities, run by committee or private ones. Being a charity is NOT a guarantee of a genuine rescue. To be a charity you have to have financial safeguards and rules for the committee. You do NOT have to have rules for how you rescue. For some reason a lot of people think that you qualify for being a charity based on how you intend to run the rescue, not how you intend to keep the bank account or appoint the committee, which is what actually happens.

- Dog Pounds. This term is associated with kennels dealing with stray dogs. There are areas all over the UK where dogs are put to sleep simply to make room for the next strays. It is a horrible job, deciding which dogs to kill, but every day a new van load comes and you have to put them somewhere. A lot of these simply sell the dogs on to anyone interested. They don't usually have the time, money or staff to homecheck and they don't want the dogs back. There is usually no history on the dogs and it is rare for the dogs to have any form of training or assessment with a few exceptions.

So how do you decide where to get your rescue dog from? I have already said it should be difficult to get a rescued dog. This is the least you should expect from the rescue:

- You should be homechecked to make sure you live where you say and not on the top floor of a block of flats.

- You should be asked to sign a lengthy adoption agreement that tells you the animal must be neutered if not already and that you can't sell or rehome it; it must be returned if you can't keep it.

- Where there is a history, it should be told to you, but you will never know the previous owner's name and address and they will never know yours.

- Even if the dog is a pedigree, you should never be given the papers. The papers themselves change hands on the black market and can end up in the hands of puppy farmers.

- You may be asked for additional identification to prove that you are who you say you are.

- If you already have a dog, a careful introduction should be made at the rescue centre and an assessment should be made as to whether the dogs seem compatible. You should NEVER be allowed to choose a dog and take it home to meet your other one.

- A donation is usually required. You are not buying the dog. You make a donation to cover the rescue centre's costs and to make dogs available for people to rehome. You will not get the donation back if you return the dog; look up the word "donation".

- You should be allowed to make more than one visit if necessary to be sure you bond with a specific dog but don't expect the rescue centre to have the same dog sitting there for days and be turning other homes away whilst you decide.

- You should expect to be guided on which dog or dogs is/are suitable. Be suspicious of kennels that allow you to wander about choosing at random like a supermarket.

- If you are told that you can't have a dog or that a particular dog isn't suitable, congratulate the rescue centre. I get fed up with saying "no" for good reasons and then listening to idiots rant on about how maybe I don't want to find homes for the dogs and isn't any home better than sitting in kennels 24 hours a day. Firstly, the dogs don't sit in a kennel all day and, secondly, no, any home is NOT better than waiting for the right home. So don't come to my rescue if you don't like my decision!

- If you are dealing with a breed rescue, make sure someone has actually met and assessed the dog and that they are not just repeating the owner's description of the dog. We've been through why already in this chapter. People are liars.

Puppy Farms

Think you know how to avoid puppy farmed dogs? Think again. Lots of my clients have puppy farmed dogs and didn't know. You do have to be slightly stupid to have done it in the first place, but it happens regularly. Quite a few clients actually knew that the dog was probably from a puppy farm and bought it anyway. After all, it's just a puppy; they think that they can put it right; how bad can it be? I'm afraid that you can't put it right and you are selfishly perpetuating the misery of these places so STOP buying from them.

Puppy farms only exist because you buy the dogs. That's it, quite simple. If they couldn't be sold, they wouldn't breed them. Don't flatter yourself by claiming you "saved" a dog. You didn't. You made space for more and condemned more dogs to death.

There are frequent adverts in most papers for kennels, advertising anything from seven to 15 breeds. Every week, same list, same dogs always available. Where exactly do you think that many dogs come from? One in my area says "we are not a puppy farm" in their advert. They are telling the truth because they didn't breed them on site but they get the puppies from the farms. Vans deliver litters week in, week out to these places and YOU are buying them. There are no parents so you have no idea what you are buying. The puppies you see are lucky in that they survived that far. Many don't. And the poor parents of those puppies are already breeding again in squalid and horrible conditions to fill the place you just made.

I know people who have fallen for the "good breeders ask us to sell their puppies" rubbish. What sort of a good breeder sells on their puppies to a kennels? In any case it is against Kennel Club rules for a third party to sell your puppies, so a good breeder wouldn't and couldn't do it. If you ask for the KC registrations or pedigree certificates before you buy, you will see the names and addresses of the breeders. These are often farms and are frequently in Wales. Go to meet the parents of your dog – if they let you in.

Some of these multiple breed outlets are big businesses and are even now referred to as "puppy supermarkets". They have flash stores and sales people. However, they are still puppy farmed puppies, however grand the shop. As long as you have the money, you can buy anything. This is one reason why they still exist. I know people who have gone and bought a puppy of a totally unsuitable breed from one of these places because all the decent breeders wouldn't sell them one.

It isn't just the multiple breed outlets that sell you a puppy farmed dog. It has become more common for individuals to buy a litter from one of these places to sell to make a profit. Of course, lies have to be told to explain the lack of a mother for the puppies. Some of these lies are well thought out, simply to stop you asking questions. Here are the ones heard most often:

- The mother of the pups got out and was run over (cue tears).

- I am selling them for a friend/relative who just happens to have a terrible terminal illness and cannot sell them him/herself.

- I bought them from a pet shop where they were being teased by children so I've saved them (you still have to pay).

Ask to see the paperwork and then ask why the "friend/relative" lives such a long way from them. Ask if you can speak to them to arrange to see the mother; after all, if the person selling them is willing to have all the puppies there to sell, surely it isn't too much to ask to have them get the mother for you? Ask for the name of their vet – surely they have one if their poor dog was run over?

I know someone who bought a West Highland White puppy from a man in a flat who had a Westie he said was the mother of puppies he was selling. He seemed very shifty and the purchaser had a good look at the adult dog. A bitch that has recently had a litter would show some signs and would have at least slightly baggy teats. This Westie was in great condition and a medical miracle as it was actually male. The purchaser contacted my rescue centre and we persuaded the man to give us all the dogs for rescue. He was not happy as he had paid £100 for each of the four puppies, expecting to sell them each for about £300–£400. What a shame.

Don't be naïve and don't be frightened to ask questions. If you want to buy a puppy that might die before it is 12 months old, have serious mental and physical problems and be part of a horrific greedy cycle, then go ahead but don't pat yourself on the back and tell people you've done the dog a favour.

There is no guarantee when you buy anything but you can improve your odds of getting a happy, healthy family pet if you ask questions and do your research. Be honest with yourself. There is no point in buying a strong assertive breed if you are a soft touch. No working breed is likely to be happy sitting in your lounge all day whilst you go to work. If you are lazy, don't buy a long-coated breed. If you have young children, don't buy a tiny breed that can be easily hurt.

With any dog you get back what you put in. So if you did your research and got a dog from a good breeder or a reputable rescue you are half way there. If you go to training classes immediately and ask for help as soon as there seems to be a problem, then you should end up with a well-behaved, safe family pet. If you don't do these things, you'll end up coming to me and I'm not nice!

4

PLAY AND TOYS

I have the luxury and privilege of specializing in German Shepherd Dogs and therefore have the opportunity to observe and train with several police forces. This means that I can see the results of actions which provoke or improve a bite and I understand how important toys can be as a training aid since this is how good forces train their working dogs. My experience has taught me that the same things, done badly or inappropriately, can cause your dog to become aggressive and bite.

The first rule is: NO play fighting of any kind, no tug of war – don't do it. I know lots of books still say you can so long as you always win. This is rubbish. You can't always win. I have yet to see a pet dog that is "played" with in this way give up items on one command and not ever want to take and hold things he shouldn't have. You can't say to a dog, "Here, try and take this off me," and then expect it respect you. If you want respect: things are yours; dogs don't offer them to their friends so neither should you. This sort of game is used to teach a correct, controllable bite in a working dog; it is not something you should do with your pet.

Certain breeds bred to work, especially dogs like terriers and lurchers, are stimulated by specific things. As they were bred to chase, catch and kill prey, that instinct is still strong in some of them. So it isn't a surprise to learn that furry and squeaky toys are a great favourite. These toys stimulate and recreate the behaviour of caught prey so these are not good toys for those breeds or any individual dog that shows an interest in killing the local dog or cat population.

If you are playing fetch with a toy, use common sense. Don't pick up the toy and tease the dog, having the dog jumping at you trying to grab the toy first. This is totally inappropriate and the dog can't distinguish between throwing itself at you to get the toy from you and throwing itself at you in other circumstances when you have something you don't want the dog to have.

If your dog likes toys, make sure some are put away. Swap a few every week to keep them interesting. Another good idea is to swap toys with other owners. Nothing interests a dog more than having a toy he thinks was stolen from another dog.

I had to sort out a serious problem between the police and a pet dog because of play of the type I have just described. A family was in the park with their pet Labrador and their kids were playing ball with it. They all thought it was really funny to tease the dog and get it to leap at them trying to grab the toy. They would throw it from one to another, driving the dog mad. Close by was another family without a dog whose two young girls were playing with a ball, throwing it between them. Of course the Lab thought it was much easier to get their ball and ran over launching himself at one of the girls. He knocked her down and in grabbing at the ball he ripped her hand open and his nails ripped her face open as he jumped on top of her on the ground. This dog had no intention of hurting this child; he had been taught by his irresponsible family that he could behave like this. The poor girl spent two days in hospital and had plastic surgery on her hand. The dog was initially seized but the family did eventually get it back after an expensive legal argument.

Q&A

My dog loves chasing rabbits and has occasionally caught one. Surely this isn't related to his serious attack on a small terrier recently?

How stupid are you? Your dog chases and kills small furry things that run. Dogs do not refer to the "Encyclopaedia of Animal Species" before deciding to chase something. If it is small and furry and runs and you have allowed him to do this, he will do it everywhere. Get some training and do not let the dog off lead until it is sorted.

My dog loves playing but won't give anything up. He enjoys teasing us. Is this OK?

Of course not. The dog isn't teasing you. He is proving a point by showing you that he isn't giving it back. Get two or three toys and, when he picks up the first one, show him the second one. When he drops the first to show an interest in the second one, retrieve the first one before throwing the other.

My dog constantly brings toys to me. Should I be flattered that he only wants to play with me?

No, you shouldn't. Your dog is bored and possibly controlling you. What does your dog have to keep him occupied? Chews, toys, bones? Something interesting to get treats out of? Do you spoil the dog and respond to demands every time? Take charge, making sure your dog is mentally occupied with things that don't always involve you.

There are some great toys on the market these days which really suit the collies and a few others. These involve sliding and popping doors to get to the treats. Whilst these are great, once learned there is no variety and the dogs get everything out quickly. Some dogs simply aren't bright enough to learn the trick or can't be bothered.

The Box Game
One of my favourite ideas (started for my beloved Sasha to give her something to do that didn't involve my shoes or furniture) is my cardboard box trick. Get a box of reasonable size, let the dog see you putting something interesting in there like a handful of biscuits or a chew. When teaching the dog the point, something smelly works best. Tape up the box, putting a small hole in the side if necessary, then give it to the dog. Sasha preferred to steal it from a kitchen work surface.

   The dog will have fun tearing up the box to get the prize. For a really clever or quick dog, you can put a smaller box inside, rattling about. The bigger box needs to have a treat in as reward, but then something better in the smaller box and so on.

   If you use a treat ball of any type, use your imagination. I usually put a few dry treats in with a few small cubes of cheese. This creates the idea that there is something better in there. Dogs often think, when real cheese comes out, that they have somehow learned the trick. Trying to work out how to get just cheese rather than simply a treat is much more interesting to a dog than simply getting the ordinary reward.

Names of Toys

Even several toys can be more interesting then you think. Your dog may be able to learn the names of several different toys. Again being sent to find a specific one is more interesting than just "fetch your toy".

To teach this, start with two toys. Make them different such as a tennis ball and a rubber bone. Keep one next to you and only throw one. You must say, "Fetch the BALL," assuming you are using the ball. Emphasize the name of the toy. Let the dog fetch it several times. Then, in your other hand, pick up the other toy so the dog can see it. Don't let the dog take it, say "No" but try not to pull the toy away. Keeping the second toy in sight, go back to throwing the first.

At some point, drop the second toy gently on the floor, and say "No" to the dog. If the dog takes it, just say "No" gently and take it back, throw the first toy, and go back to the "Fetch the ball" bit. Keep this going until the dog ignores the dropped toy and fetches the ball.

When this is reliable, throw both together, only throwing the second toy gently, giving a clear command for the ball. Wave the dog away from the second if necessary and send him for the ball. When this is reliable, throw the second a little further each time, keeping the ball command clear. You may want to spread this over several training sessions, I am describing the whole process here.

The next step is to put the ball out of sight and use the second toy. Change the command, of course, maybe to "Fetch the bone." A few retrieves, then introduce the ball as the second toy, repeating as above.

Gradually you should be able to throw both toys, giving the command for just one. It helps to wave the dog to the right one. When the dog is happy with this, introduce a third toy, using the process for first and exchanging third for second as above.

This makes fetching a toy to play with much more challenging and stimulating. You can even plant the target toy somewhere a bit more difficult before you ask.

The Plant Pot Game

Most dogs love to find things – especially if they're tasty. Using their natural reaction to finding food, you can make a good game. Invest in several plastic plant pots and some smelly treats.

To start with you have to do a sort of Tommy Cooper routine (younger readers, Google him!). Show the dog the treat, lifting the treat in one hand, plant pot in the other. Put the treat down under the pot and encourage the dog to work out how to get it. Some dogs use a very quick "flick" technique to turn the pot over, some chase it all over before bashing it against a firm surface where they can pick it up or squash it.

I teach this using a "find it" command. You'll see why in a minute once we start extending the game.

Get another plant pot, letting the dog see which one you put it under and let the dog get it. Gradually do this, swapping the pots around a bit like in those fairground trick cons. You can then put a few outside together with only one having the treat.

Once the dog gets the hang of this properly, you can make a bigger game. Place the pots in different places around the garden, some more hidden than others. Ask the dog to "find it" and send it off round the garden to work out which one has the treat. By retrieving the pots at the end of the game and putting them in different places, this game is new every time.

The Obedience Game

Some dogs obey commands very slowly – almost in slow motion, waiting for you to give up before they have to do it completely. I devised a play version of this that usually speeds it up.

Get the dog to sit. It doesn't matter how long it takes, just get the proper sit. Once the dog does it, quickly tap the dog, saying "Go" and run away. Dogs usually run after you; praise the dog when it does. Stop, get the *sit* again and repeat this a few times. You are trying to change the end result to something really fun.

You can do this with a *down* too. Same process, tap the dog and run as soon as the dog obeys.

Once the dog speeds up with the command, you need to teach a *stay* or *wait*, keeping your hand up as a signal, like stopping traffic. Take a step away before waving your hand and running away giving the *go* signal. The whole process then becomes more fun. The dog wants to obey quicker to get to the game part faster. Use the extra focus from the dog to make it wait a bit longer. Start getting a *sit* and then a *down* or vice versa before playing.

It is better to use your dog's play drive than to keep on and on with treats or pushing. This way you and the dog have fun and you create the desire to cooperate. This is really the principle of training generally, but some dogs of stronger personalities still need a bit more persuading.

You can use agility play as a way of tiring and training your dog. Even a dog with joint problems can usually do the tunnel, see saw and weave poles. Just use your imagination and have fun!

5

CASE STUDIES

In this chapter we will look at a couple of more unusual cases in a more clinical style.

Dog: Female Samoyed, 6 years old, spayed
Noushka came into my rescue after being removed from a shed in which she had lived for two years. Having bitten two people in her foster home, she needed to be safe in kennels. I guessed, correctly, that she was originally puppy farmed. Noushka bit randomly and, if she started, she would keep biting, no backing off and threatening.

For the last two years she was owned by an older man who couldn't cope with her biting and shut her away. Prior to that she was owned by a family with kids who felt her to be a danger to their children. They had taken her to many classes, but as a puppy farmed dog, she was mentally unstable.

After three months in kennels, nothing had changed. She was on food free from any additives, had a stable routine and had no interest in toys or treats. She veered from ignoring you to suddenly lunging and spent most of her day in her run screaming at anything that happened. Whilst seeming to want to come out, she would only ever go about 15 feet, then race back and bite you if you were in the way; walks involved dragging her.

Three months in, there was no change. I was bitten six times by her; it would have been more if I wasn't quicker. She simply lived in her own world and I suggested to the rescue that they put her down. Whilst she could be petted and she occasionally wagged her tail, she never made eye contact or acknowledged me and I was the only person walking her. I felt there was no hope. Unless I could make a connection, I couldn't influence her and she was a dog that could be wound up very easily.

I had been offered some training in the use of Bach Flower Remedies, and was highly sceptical. I hated homeopathy. It made no sense to me, but I accepted the training as the remedies were natural products and couldn't hurt. Despite my misgivings, as I'd been through obedience, food, routine, gestures, body language and play with Noushka, I started using the remedies since there were no conventional methods left to me.

Noushka was treated with five remedies which I felt reflected her emotional issues: treated in her water and on a treat three times daily, approximately two drops of each. After having had to sedate and muzzle her previously to tidy up her dirty coat during which she cut my head open after smacking me into a wall, I didn't hold out much hope. I gave her Vine, Walnut, Cherry Plum, Impatiens and Vervain.

Her routine and feeding were unchanged. For ten days there was no difference. On Day 11 the first sign appeared that there might be a change. Instead of charging back to the kennels after 15 feet of the walk in the paddock, she carried on and wandered around on the grass for about ten minutes before running back. Over the next few days this time increased by around ten minutes a day.

After 14 days she was moulting – the huge undercoat comes out in large tufts that can normally be pulled by hand. Her previous behaviour had meant that to do it this time I would need her to be knocked out. However, I felt that she was more stable and she seemed more relaxed so when I saw these enticing tufts I pulled a couple. There was no reaction at all. I continued pulling down her back leg but near her hock it must have been a bit matted as when I pulled I felt it pull her skin. My reaction was to throw up my arm in the way to avoid her biting my face as she swung round. She did no more than air snap as in fairness I had hurt her, then she turned away. I was thrilled.

These changes continued for six weeks, ending up with a dog who recognized me, played with toys, liked meeting people, wagged her tail and instigated affection. She was put up for adoption after 12 weeks and rehomed after another four. Noushka remained on Remedies at full strength for two months after rehoming, then half strength for a month then no more. She lived out the rest of her life within a few boundaries in terms of not being allowed to pester or bully for what she wanted and she even made a doggy friend.

Dog: Echo, 4-year-old English Springer Spaniel (ESS)
Echo was a rescue dog, owned for 18 months by a couple in their thirties with no children. Not much was known of his history. The couple had another ESS, Billy, a male of two years old that they had got as a young puppy. Both dogs were castrated.

Echo was a slightly manic dog. Like a lot of his breed, he was a busy dog with lots of energy and easily bored and distracted. His problem though was an unexpected attack. He flew, biting and threatening at his owners. It was usually at specific moments: walking into the kitchen if he was already there, putting his lead on or off, stroking him. It was not every time and two previous trainers had given up.

I had changed his food to something free from any artificial products in case they affected him, but nothing happened. Billy had also started copying Echo. The lady owner had stopped having anything to do with Echo as she was afraid of him.

Although Echo liked treats, his easily distracted behaviour meant focusing was difficult. The same with toys; he loved toys but other things could be just as interesting. I felt Echo needed very short routines, gradually adding to them.

I started with the basics of *sit*, *down* and *come here*. All rewarded with a treat. I spent five hours with them all at home initially, setting a timescale for moving on over the next two weeks.

The next stage was to teach Echo to come out of the kitchen when asked, reward with a treat and make him stay whilst the human went into the kitchen. There had never been a bite if he wasn't in the kitchen first. The *stay* was built up slowly as he lost interest within a few seconds. If he tried to follow a person into the kitchen, he was taught to stop at the door, to end with being called into the kitchen for a reward.

The last part was control over his affection. I asked them to call him frequently, but only to give a few strokes, then send him away. This built up in terms of the length of time contact was made, always ending with him being sent away.

The overall effect was a much calmer dog. As he now had firm boundaries and affection but no gaps he could bully or manipulate in, he relaxed in between actions for the first time ever. The lady owner even started walking him again and playing. Over about three months the strictness of some rules relaxed and Echo became a much better dog. Billy, without the influence of Echo, simply turned back into a good dog.

Dog: Kai, German Shepherd Dog, 18 months old, castrated

Kai was bred by an irresponsible person who couldn't sell him as his ears were soft. For the first 12 months of his life he lived in a kennel and had never been off the property. He was then sold to a lovely but unsuspecting lady whose boss had given her permission to have a dog at work in her small private office.

The owner had recently come out of a long relationship and so the first few weeks with the dog involved a lot of crying and cuddling – the last thing an unsocialized, arrogant adolescent GSD needs. At first he allowed anyone in the house, especially her father who he saw most days. Gradually his behaviour got worse: barking at passers-by from the window, threatening visitors, lunging at people and dogs in the street. The last straw was when he bit the father on a visit. The owner said she had to hang onto fence and lamp posts to stop him getting away from her.

At work he stopped people coming into the office and had to be tied to a radiator as he was trying to bite workmates. On two occasions he did actually bite people, including the MD. Although interested in toys and food, Kai was far more interested in lunging and controlling and scaring people. His owner did all sorts of obedience and classes with him. In a class he eventually settled, but could suddenly kick off. He became what I call a "vampire dog" – only going out at dusk and dawn to avoid people.

It was obvious Kai was a high-drive dog – lots of energy, can't keep still. Clever but with not enough to do, and with an owner who felt guilty about now having to leave him at home and who then overcompensated when she was home.

Basic rules had to be introduced. No getting on beds or furniture without invitation. Walking in a head collar to gain control of his weight and attitude. The owner was coached into much stronger body language. No going around the dog, but walking confidently. Big hand signals, more stepping into the dog's space. Kai was also taught to step back from the door by his owner. This was done by getting the owner to move in front of the dog, back to the door, facing the dog. Using a stepping action and hand signal, the dog was taught to step back out of the space, then made to wait. All this was done initially with nobody at the door. An important lesson with training: break down the process into easy bits. Make sure the dog knows what you want before bringing in the distraction or stimulus. You can't teach the action with the problem there.

The background training to this was my "toy therapy". You have to find a toy the dog would give anything for. For Kai this was easy, a toy on a rope was his favourite thing. Where a dog isn't bothered, a process of carrying, teasing playing and excluding the dog usually gets it going. The owner's job is to keep producing the toy, throwing it in the air, kissing it, swinging it, but not letting the dog have it. It is never left out. The dog must only see it as an object of desire and really want to get it.

Once Kai was going totally bonkers over the toy, he was ready for an unknown visitor. My assistant in his case. His owner sent him back from the door. The visitor could be seen through the frosted glass, swinging the toy. Kai very quickly focused on this and when the door was opened, went mad for the toy, which was thrown by the visitor. He retrieved it and gave it back to the visitor who threw it again. After being allowed to play on his own with it for five minutes, it was put away.

This ended with having toys hanging outside the office door and the same process used there. This was a great success. Kai now wanted as many visitors as possible and even whined when people just passed by. Gradually over around three months, the toy was used sporadically, but by then he realized he quite liked people.

These cases are just an overview of common types of problems. There is no one way to train a dog; it has to be done on an individual basis. We learn new things all the time, so always ask for some help.

6

RELATIONSHIP AND CONTROL

Firstly, let me tell you what I tell all my clients: you as the owner are half the problem and half the solution.

If you are perfect and haven't made a single mistake, then your dog is mentally ill and nobody can help you. Harsh? Yes, probably, but true. If you think you are perfect nobody can help you! I don't accept every job I am offered. I do turn clients away who talk only about the dog's behaviour and don't mention themselves.

Change in the owners is the only way forward. Unless respect can be maintained, no dog does what you say. It isn't just a question of the dog knowing what the command means, the dog must want to do it for you. If you change, so does the dog. My beloved first German Shepherd, Sasha, was the most special dog. Not a bad bone in her body, I still miss her. When I got her she was my only dog and, of course, her training benefited from that fact. I only had to find time for her. She was very special, kind and gentle and willing apart from her "GSD moments" when she would defy me, just to see what I was going to do. I could speak to her in a normal voice and she obeyed every-thing. If she was across the paddock from me, I just had to call her and I could turn and continue my conversation knowing she would still be coming. You hardly knew you had her, she was amazing and there will never be another like her.

When Sasha was about five or six, she suddenly didn't go out one afternoon when I opened the door to let the dogs into the garden. By then I had five dogs. I looked into the lounge and she was just standing there with a strange expression. As I went towards her, she fell over. It turned out she had spondylosis. This is arthritis of the spine where bone spurs grow out and meet the next vertebrae and fuse them together. It can be painful and debilitating and an x-ray showed at least six affected, five already fused. This was unbelievable. Sasha did agility and had been doing so a few days previously. Nobody had realized how bad she was.

Sasha effectively retired that day. She still did some obedience, and I was lucky still to have her at age 10 when she finally couldn't deal with the condition. To say it broke my heart to lose her is an understatement. I was very privileged to have known her.

The change in her was gradual at first. I was just so glad still to have my dog that I didn't notice I had gone a bit soft with her. If she went a bit more slowly into position, well that was fine, she was sometimes uncomfortable. However, she had been an exceptionally well-mannered dog and very obedient and was wonderful with animals, kids and people. About a year after her back problem happened, I had her loose in the paddock as I was talking to clients and I had told her she could wander off. There came a moment when I needed her to illustrate a point and as usual I just called gently across to her to come back. I turned and continued my explanations to the client and then picked up my lead and twisted round to put it on my dog. Except there was no dog.

Sasha was about half-way back, sniffing around quite happily. I was amazed and called her and she came, wagging her tail happily and I swear she was laughing.

Over the next few months this became a common behaviour and other things became less reliable too. I often had to use a slightly sterner voice with her. It wasn't the speed of reaction, slowing down was understandable, it was the defiance. She would stand and glare at me, and when I told her to do something, she would just laugh and trot off.

She made me laugh out loud sometimes – my lovely girl was so naughty! So what made her be like this? The answer was *me*. I had changed. I didn't reinforce commands properly, I didn't follow through if she didn't do something, I didn't tell her off. I was just so glad to still have her in my life I let her get away with murder. With a dog who had the most wonderful nature, it wasn't an issue. Had she been a dog with a dodgy attitude and any aggressive tendencies, it might have been very different.

The point is this was an exceptionally well behaved dog that stopped being so well behaved. The boundaries in our relationship became unclear and loose and she took advantage of it. In her case as a dog with a superb temperament, the consequences were just a nuisance. In the case of a dog with aggression related problems, this lack of control on my part might have meant the dog being destroyed.

I am telling you this story to illustrate something I say often. There is no such thing as a trained dog. A dog may know all the words, but that doesn't mean it will do it for *you*.

The word "dominance" has become a dirty word in dog training. Some trendy trainers say it is now to be called "natural behaviour". Being a trendy trainer does not make you knowledgeable. Copying the latest words and using the latest gadgets are things lots of inexperienced trainers do to make themselves look better. Or so they think. It has also become a very bitchy industry with a huge number of very poor quality trainers and behaviourists constantly criticizing other people's work – usually people far more successful than they are. If you want to find a trainer or behaviourist, then don't judge them on how much jargon they know or on their repetition of other people's ideas. Judge their work, speak to clients who have been through the process with them, find out if they actually have any successful cases; you may be surprised!

I don't care what the latest word is, or the fact that some trainers are saying that the pack structure doesn't exist. They are wrong. I live with several dogs and cats. My dogs live indoors, sleep in the bedroom (I can see lots of you smiling at that) and there is a definite pecking order. At the point of writing this, my 12-month-old GSD bitch is pushing the older GSD bitch very hard. She is coming into an important period of psychological growth and change and is very obviously trying to take over and several disagreements are breaking out.

Dogs like consistency and boundaries. They like affection and company. Humans like these things too and, where they don't exist, both dogs and humans struggle to understand where they fit in and what is expected. A dog wants the same rules and boundaries every day, it feels secure with this. Your whole household must have the same rules and boundaries or the dog will make mistakes with some members and be punished or at least stressed and confused. It is amazing how many families have dogs and argue constantly about where the dog is sleeping or if it can go on the sofa. Decide all of this before you get a dog and if you can't agree, don't get one.

As I said earlier, even if I think I can train the dog, if the people won't be trained I turn them away. A couple with a five-year-old son were once waiting for me in the car park. They had a 12-month-old crossbreed male that had bitten the child and also a visitor. As I was chatting to them in the car park, the dog was in the car. The child was standing next to his mother. All the time we were talking the child kept kicking his mother and pulling at her clothes. At first it wasn't too hard but after a short while he kicked her very hard and she squealed.

Mum pushed the child away and said in a pathetic voice, "Now Charlie, you mustn't kick Mummy."

Charlie, of course, simply pulled a face and continued with the kicking and pulling. She told him again in the same way and I looked at the father and asked why he wasn't doing anything about it.

"My wife can deal with him perfectly well. Why should I do it?" he said, looking away across the car park.

I patiently (OK not that patiently) explained that it might do the kid some good to see a united front rather than seeing a father who didn't care how he treated his mother, didn't he realize that the kid thought he was supporting him?

"Oh, he knows I don't approve," he said with what he thought was a menacing stare but just looked like someone who had forgotten his glasses.

I was intrigued.

"How does he know, is he psychic?" I asked facetiously.

"No, I just give him a 'look' and he knows immediately."

Brilliant, I thought, I must see this.

"OK. Do it now and stop him then," I challenged.

"But I am doing it," he said in a big voice.

"Your child must be blind then," I said sadly.

Of course, the point here is that if they couldn't set any boundaries for the child what chance did the dog have? If the kid kicked his mother like that what the hell was he doing to the dog? The only surprise was that the dog hadn't bitten him repeatedly. We got the dog out of the car and he was lovely. I felt quite upset seeing this poor dog with this idiot family.

I did a simple temperament test and the dog passed it, no problem at all. As I finished this and was trying to explain to them, the kid kicked his mother hard, again. I lost it this time and leant over to him and screamed "*Stop it, now!*" in his face. He jumped back like a rabbit and stood perfectly still. Father wasn't amused.

"Really there's no need for that. We don't speak to him like that."

"Maybe you should. He has actually stopped hurting his mother for the first time since you got here. Exactly how many times does he get to hurt her before someone actually does something?"

We continued to talk and I told them that the dog was fine; it was they who were mad. I said that they were lucky this was such a nice dog as most would have taken the face off their child if he treated them like he treats his mother. I begged them to give me the dog so I could rehome him, I couldn't bear to let him go back.

At this point the child, who didn't now dare to kick his mother or come too close to us, picked up some large stones and threw them at his mother and the last one at the dog. I saw it coming and pulled the dog away and put my leg out, catching the stone. Mother's hit her; she could sort herself out.

To my utter amazement the father just turned round and said, "We're wasting our time here. Let's go. This woman obviously blames us and not the dog."

He reached to take the lead and I said, "No." A big row broke out and I said if they took the dog I would call the police and the RSPCA and do everything I could to get the dog off them. They eventually gave up as I was really mad and drove off. I got a letter from them asking when they could have their dog back and threatening legal action. I heard no more after I reminded them that the car park had a surveillance camera and the whole fiasco was on film.

Nobody can train just the dog. If people won't learn, won't accept criticism or change, then the dog will behave in just the same way as it did before training.

Getting respect from your dog doesn't have to mean creating challenges all the time. One of my favourite tricks that I developed is something I call "backwards training". This is a great way of looking like you have far more power than you do without doing much. This means it is a good way for kids to show leadership over their dog. Each time the dog does something that fits a command, such as comes into the lounge and lies down, you point to the floor and say, "Good dog, down," as if you thought of it. Point to where the dog actually is, not at your own feet or the dog is likely to come over to that spot. Do the same thing if it sits: raise your hand and give the command, say "Come here," if the dog comes to you voluntarily. This system is meant to be used if you are having a problem with your dog. If your dog has been showing some aggression, or simply doesn't listen to anyone, this takes away a lot of the dog's power.

Some dogs get a bit annoyed with it! I know a dog that would walk round for ages before finally giving in and lying down. As he did he gave the owners a look as if to say, "Go on, get it over with." You must say the "good dog" as well as the command or the dog won't feel it has done the right thing.

In general you must follow through a command. Don't say one if you have no intention of making sure the dog does it. Dogs are good at learning that you will shout "lie down" at least ten times before getting up and doing something about it. So they just wait and often you lose interest or get annoyed before the tenth time and give up so the dog wins. Say it once, then go to do something about it in the right way. Always praise the dog for doing what you want.

If someone starts a command, he must finish it. Tempting as it is for you to get up and help out or start shouting at the dog, don't do it. The dog must learn that each person has the same standards and will reinforce what he says.

Use the same rule if you have a dog that tends to run to the soft touch of the family to get out of doing something. If the dog is being told to do something, everybody else stays out of it. Don't look at the dog, don't speak to the dog. Teach it that it must respect everyone just the same.

There are rules you should follow that are based on a simple premise: if your dog did what it does to you to another dog what would the consequence be? If your dog walked over to another dog and sat on top of it, would the other dog kiss him and think he is lovely? Would the other dog laugh and be flattered at the attention? Of course not. The first dog is likely to get up and bite your dog. Does a dog allow another dog to sit drooling over him when he is eating and constantly paw at him to get the food? No and again if he did he would get bitten. Yet owners allow these things and then wonder why the same dog runs off when let loose or bites visitors when they come.

Whilst we now know that the pack structure is more fluid than first thought and some domestic dogs aren't particularly bothered about position, a lot are. Don't call it dominance or pack leadership, call it respect and consistency.

A dog is born on a mental ladder. Breed, early experience, ancestors and circumstances mean that when you get your dog, it is already on a rung of the ladder. Look at the ladder as something you are standing on too except you should be at the top, looking down. A dog born with a naturally submissive and gentle character is on a low rung of the ladder, a dog from a strong-minded working breed is higher up. So if you get a dog and make mistakes, your dog climbs the ladder. If he started from a low point your dog may just be a bit disrespectful and a bit of a nuisance. If he was born higher up mentally, he is more likely to be aggressive to get control as he climbs up almost as high or higher than you. Of course, some badly bred dogs can have mental problems totally unrelated to dominance and these are generalizations, but the overall point is important. So this is why you can have one dog that you make mistakes with and it becomes an aggressive, difficult dog that you become afraid of and why you can do the same things with a different dog and nothing serious happens. Each dog is different.

It is very frustrating for owners with dogs who behave badly outside to be told by other dog owners how to train their dog. Everybody is an expert in the local park. What they are telling you is how they trained *their dog*, not yours. They always think if only they had the lead the dog would be fine. One lady I know was so furious at the comments about her Rottweiler who lunged at other dogs that she told one know-it-all who constantly berated her in the park to walk the dog himself. She said it was very satisfying to see this fool dragged through a lovely patch of mud by her galloping dog. When she retrieved the dog he had suddenly decided that the dog, who previously he had described as a "man's dog" that couldn't be trained by a woman, as a psycho that needed to be put to sleep. His tirade might have been more effective if the assembled crowd hadn't been laughing at the dog poop sliding down his face.

- Don't give commands if you have no intention of following them up.

- Don't share your food or let your dog stare and drool while you are eating.

- Enjoy your dog, be affectionate but don't keep responding to a rude dog that is always pawing and barking for attention.

- Don't let your dog lie on your feet or stand on you, especially when you are petting it.

- Don't let your dog jump on the sofa or beds unless it is by command.

- Don't let your dog sit on you with its paws on your shoulders staring you in the face. How dominant is that, are you mad?

- Don't allow jumping up or charging through doors.

- Don't put your dog's lead on if it involves wrestling to get the dog to stand still long enough to get it attached. Get some help.

- Don't allow any sort of growling or mouthing. It isn't mouthing or playing – it is biting.

- Never play fight, wrestle or play any sort of tug of war – not even if you think you win. You don't. Read the other chapters.

A lady with a Chihuahua that bit like an alligator once told me that she really couldn't understand why people where she lived couldn't control their dogs and that a German Shepherd near her constantly barked aggressively at them whenever she was walking her dog. I pointed out that it was actually her dog that always barked first and was the cause of the problem. Her answer was that it didn't matter because she picked it up and why couldn't this other owner do something. I got one of my Shepherds and asked if she would pick it up . . .

7

PROBLEMS

There are lots of books on the market covering obedience training. Most owners know the basics already. However, I want to touch on exactly why some dogs know the words but don't want to do it. The chapter about your relationship with your dog is relevant to this section too. A well behaved dog is the result of consistent training, but also a dog that wants to please you and is willing to accept your commands. If your dog doesn't respect you, all the obedience training in the world will never make the dog do what you say. Go to any good training class and watch what happens when the trainer picks up the lead of the most unruly dog there. Within a few seconds the dog simply stands or sits and just waits to see what to do next. The trainer looks like and sounds like the boss so the dog waits for instructions.

I do not personally train with food, I never have apart from things like training discs which need food as part of the process of bonding the dog to the purpose of the noise. I do not want any dog to be in a position of having a method for making me give up food which is what most food training does. If you pick up food and your dog sits before you speak, you have not taught "sit" you have taught "give me food". Dogs do not give up their food to other dogs no matter how nice a gesture the other dog has made. I also do not use any form of "shock" collar or gadget. I was told by several trainers when I was young and learning that I would never be able to retrain a livestock killer without using electric shock collars. I have proved this wrong repeatedly.

So, with any problem that you have, your starting point has to be making sure your dog is respectful, of good health and has good basic obedience. Without this all the clever methods and gadgets in the world will make no difference. Any sudden change in behaviour or character should be checked out first by your vet.

Nervousness
I have put this first in this chapter as it is the root of other evils. Most owners of aggressive dogs much prefer to describe their dogs as having "nervous aggression" as somehow they think this is preferable to being just plain nasty. It is rare indeed for me to treat a nervous dog that is anywhere near as nervous as first impressions would indicate. In the huge majority of cases, the dog has learned to react nervously to get out of things it doesn't like.

If you have a dog that cowers when you or others stroke it, then don't touch the dog when it cowers away. Gesture as if you are going to touch it, then when the dog drops away, lift your hand a few inches above the dog's head. Use a calm and friendly voice and keep talking until the dog lifts its head to your hand. Small distances at first, but the dog has to learn to lift its head to get attention other-wise why would it stop doing it? Just getting the dog to stay upright and get petted makes the dog feel more confident. Don't you feel more in control when standing rather than sitting? By constantly going down to the dog you are simply rewarding the behaviour and the dog never gets better.

If your dog is afraid of noise, try to identify the type. There are some good CDs on the market with a range of sounds that you can use. Play them at the lowest possible level that just gets a reaction from your dog. Use a strong, assertive kind voice, reassuring the dog all is well. Don't touch the dog. Stand up if the dog paws at you, walk around, keep talking. Don't do it for long, turn it off then fuss the dog. Keep repeating at gradually louder volume until the dog can tolerate it better.

I have had some good results with using homeopathic treatments for noise sensitivity; as a background to your training they can make the dog feel a lot better. Natural Flower Remedies can make a big difference. Also Zylkene has improved a lot of dogs.

If your dog tends to run and hide from visitors, two things are worth trying. It seems hard on the dog to stop it from escaping, but you must. A cage in the main room is a good idea. Cover it with a blanket at first. Give it lots of reassuring voice and eye contact. If the dog will tolerate it, get the visitor to go to the cage and give a treat, something really tasty. Gradually fold the blanket back, either during a visit, if the dog is coping, or over several visits if not.

If you prefer, put the dog on a lead and, again, no petting. Use the lead to stop the dog leaving and use your voice to tell the dog you are dealing with the situation and there is nothing to worry about. Don't use a "baby voice"; this sounds like stress to the dog. Sound confident and sure of yourself. Again when the dog is ready, get visitors to stand up and offer a treat. Build that up to the visitor coming over to the dog and giving a treat. Go at your own pace, but ask for a tiny bit more each time.

If your dog is very nervous and has no confidence, and can't bear to be anywhere without you, you have probably caused that yourself. There are people who really enjoy having a needy dog that can't face life without being next to them 24 hours a day. These poor dogs won't eat without the owner, sit and cry all day when they go out, can't be left in a room without screaming and banging the door; it's criminal.

If you have a dog that is not that confident, your job is to help it become more confident and so be able to live a life without so much stress. It is not your job to enjoy the dog's obsession and reward it. When you are at home with your dog, come in and be cool at first. Speak to the dog – it doesn't need to feel rejected – but don't touch or pick up the dog until the initial anxiousness has passed. If anything happens that worries the dog, put it on the floor if it isn't already there and use the confident voice, no touching, and get up and walk around if the dog paws anxiously. Once the crisis has passed, carry on as normal. When you leave the room, just go, closing the door. Ignore any noise. Be firm. Come back in as before, straight in, say "Hi dog". Don't look at or touch the dog. Sit down and ignore the dog until it is calm, then call it and make a fuss. Don't allow the dog unlimited access to you and expect it to cope when you leave.

Call the dog often and make a fuss of it but don't allow it to keep pestering you, whining and pushing to keep your attention on it. Don't let it keep sitting with or on top of you. Let the dog up by invitation only. Don't say yes when it is asking, and turf it off regularly.

Barking
The commonest and most annoying problem of all, especially as this is one that gets you into serious trouble with

> • If your dog is nervous of or over-reacts to noise, leave a TV or radio on to mask background noise. Get behavioural help to desensitize the dog to the noise.
> • Don't allow a dog lacking in confidence to be with you every second and get attention on demand. Be sensible and help the dog to live with less stress.
> • Think about using a background treatment of homeopathic remedies.

other people and authorities. For some reason, stupid owners think it is really funny to persuade their dog to bark. They sit around in hysterics whilst shouting things like "Who's there?" or "Where's that cat?" Then when the dog barks at everything, they shout and scream at the dog and try to punish it. So the first lesson is: stop making your dog bark. All barking is to be discouraged, even barking at the door. The second lesson is to know why your dog is barking. Some do it out of boredom and frustration, some are dominant and object to being left, some lack confidence and have been kept that way by needy owners, some are aggressive and react to passing people and dogs, some are sensitive to sound or light. Without establishing why your dog does it, you cannot treat it since the barking can be a symptom of another problem.

There are several gadgets on the market specifically made to deter barking. Some fit on collars, some are stand-alone devices. The main ones emit an ultrasonic noise like a sharp beep when the dog barks or squirt an unpleasant smell. As they are noise-activated, be careful where you site them if using the stand-alone versions since outside noise may trigger them. Always follow the instructions carefully and use them at first whilst you are there to gauge the dog's reaction. If using the stand-alone or hand-held versions, *always* say "Good dog" as soon as the dog stops barking. If the dog gets more attention for barking than not barking, it will start again. As the dog improves, watch for the dog getting up and thinking about it but choosing not to bark. For instance, if your dog barks at the window, but training stops it, the dog will probably run to the window and then stand looking at you, waiting for the praise. If you don't reward this or don't notice, the dog will bark to get attention. So if the dog makes a good decision, tell him so!

Separation Anxiety

I have put this topic next as the first two often go hand in hand with this. True separation anxiety (SA) is *very* rare. Most dogs I see that allegedly have it have nothing of the sort. They are often ill-mannered, untrained dogs who think their owners are there simply for their amusement and refuse to be left behind. They are often dogs who have total access to the house and people when they are home and are expected to change from being with the owners every second and being doted on to being totally alone. So you may need to use the sections on nervousness and barking to get rid of the problem rather than treating a dog that can't live without you.

True separation anxiety means a dog that really has no self-confidence of any kind that just can't cope alone or cope with most circumstances. Remember wolves are not solitary animals and some dogs just cannot cope without someone with them; even another dog can help. Very few dogs fit this category and treatment for SA is often unsuccessful because of this.

There are plug-in diffusers that can help as they give off soothing hormones, and again natural remedies can work. But you must also follow the advice on nervousness to give

- If your dog is nervous, use the advice already given to help the dog to cope without you.

- Don't allow or encourage any barking; this makes no difference to your dog's ability to let you know that burglars are about.

- Give a firm command "That's enough" or "Be quiet". Always say "Good dog" once the dog is quiet.

- Leave background noise on if your dog barks at outside noises.

- Make sure your dog has plenty to do. Having 20 toys is not interesting if the same 20 are on the floor all day. Have five or six and swap them round regularly.

- Think about toys that have holes in them to put treats or food in. These can occupy the dog for hours. Make sure this toy is only available when you are out; pick it up and put it away every time you come home.

- Not all gadgets work on all dogs. Sometimes you have to try a few before the right reaction can be produced.

- If your dog is sensitive to a specific noise, buy a sound-effect CD and use it to gradually build up the dog's tolerance.

your dog the tools to gain confidence and not live like that for ever.

Sadly some owners enjoy what they see as their dog "needing" them so much. I have treated cases where owners have been actually disappointed when the dog got better and more independent. One lady confessed to stopping the homeopathic treatment as she wanted the dog to get "just a

- Build up time alone slowly.

- Use a plug-in diffuser from your vet if you feel the dog is genuinely anxious at being left rather than annoyed.

- Be calm when you return. Talk sensibly but don't pick up a panicking dog or one that is jumping up and scratching at your legs. No contact until the dog has settled down, just use your voice.

- Leave background noise on.

- Use a natural product such as Zylkene to reduce stress levels for the dog.

- Leave calmly. Don't upset the dog by over petting and using a stupid voice saying, "Mummy won't be long, *please* be good." This just makes it sound like there is something to worry about.

- You could use a dog walker to break up the dog's time alone, or use a local boarding kennels as lots do "day boarding" for working or busy owners.

- Don't get another dog. They are likely to both become anxious unless your dog used to have company and hasn't now and the behaviour only started since it has been alone. Even then, be careful.

bit better". I told her to rehome the dog and buy a teddy bear as she was the most selfish woman I had ever met.

Successful treatment means a good balance between supporting but not encouraging the behaviour. You may need a back-up of homeopathic treatment and/or a diffuser which your vet can help with. Build up the length of time your dog is alone as far as this is possible. Some dogs do feel better if you use a crate and have it covered with a blanket to simulate a secure den.

Chewing

I can't believe how many people get rid of their dogs because they are chewing. I have lost pieces of furniture, expensive clothes and shoes, irreplaceable items of sentimental value, nice gardens, toys and lots of phones and remotes. Chewing is a temporary state that can go on a long time, but can be contained to a point. I have never given up a dog for destroying my house. There is nothing I own, no matter what its value, that can ever mean more to me than my dog.

I am not a saint. I too have come home and cried when I have seen my house wrecked. My oldest dog once ate a pair of shoes. Not just any shoes. The most expensive shoes I have ever bought, ever in my life. Black patent leather, they were gorgeous and took weeks of saving to buy. I wore them to a fancy party and came home drunk. They got thrown on the floor of the bedroom with my clothes as I fell into bed and the next morning Mitch had eaten them. I sobbed and sobbed as I could never afford to replace them. He also ate through three mattresses on my bed, but that's another story. I was mad as hell and cried all day, but at no point did it cross my mind to get rid of him.

Crate training for young dogs is a great way of controlling what they chew. It is also much safer to keep the dogs away from electric cables, chemicals and sharp objects. There are lots of dogs killed by chewing the wrong things. It's better to be safe than sorry. Clients who refused to use a cage with their very young and over excitable Springer lost him when he found paracetamol in a cupboard and swallowed the whole packet. He survived the initial stomach pump but died a few days later from liver failure. The tablets weren't in a bottom cupboard either so don't think you can leave things high and they will be OK.

You know the dog will chew, so you must provide something suitable. Having several things that get swapped every day is better than 10 things always available. Here are some of my favourite and most successful methods:

- Get cardboard boxes from your local supermarket. Inside put a chew or smelly treat (or several) and tape up the box. Poke a hole in to let the smell out and leave your dog with it. You will come home to a pile of soggy cardboard but rather that than pieces of your home. If the dog gets too good at it, arrange it like "Russian dolls" with one box inside another.

- Use a toy that allows you to put treats inside and has a small hole to let them out again. Only give the toy to the dog when you go out and always pick it up when you come in. Use your imagination. It is more interesting to have a handful of dry food in it and a couple of small cubes of cheese than dry food alone. Clever dogs get more out of this as they really want the cheese and think there is some sort of trick to getting it out instead of the boring food!

- You could try giving the dog a large new bone or chew before you leave. Again take it away when you come home. Any item is more interesting when you realize you only have it for a limited time each day.

- Don't go and get another dog to solve chewing problems. They will probably just both do it.

House Training

This is sadly a common reason why dogs end up in rescue. It is a difficult thing to live with and can drive you to tears but I have never given a dog up because it was dirty. Some owners have totally unrealistic expectations about the length of time a dog can be left and not toilet. Different dogs at different ages will have different toilet habits. Don't get a puppy if you are out working all day and expect it to cope until maybe you pop in at lunchtime or go home at night. There is no way a puppy can be clean that long. Even some adults can't hold it for too long.

The classic way to house train a puppy is to put newspaper by the back door and praise the dog every time it goes there. Then after anything from a few days to a few weeks you expect the dog to stop doing that and go outside. How does the dog know the difference? Do you really think the dog can distinguish the fact that the newspaper is only there to hold the mess, not as a permanent toilet?

I only use newspaper as a "keep the mess here" aid. If a dog goes on it I just say "Good dog" calmly, with no big fuss. I take all dogs outside regularly and right from the start the big fuss is made when they do it outside. You have to go out and *stand with* the dog for a long time, not just once or twice and then think the dog understands – it doesn't. You have to be there to keep reinforcing the "Good dog" bit when the dog toilets for weeks, sometimes months.

I got a call recently from people with a nervous six-month-old dog that wasn't house trained. After the first few times they simply put him out and left him there. They admitted he ran around looking scared and he was not that confident outdoors but still didn't get the fact that he needed them to be there to reassure him. He would run in and mess in the kitchen, poor dog. When I told them they had to go out with him, the lady said:

"But it's *cold* outside."

"Buy a cat then," I replied.

One lady once rang me about a three-year-old Golden Retriever bitch that had always been dirty overnight since a puppy and sometimes during the day. Her husband was so fed up he wanted rid of the dog and she was distraught. The root of the problem was that they were convinced the dog felt guilty when they either came down in the morning or returned after work as the dog slunk around the edges of the kitchen and rolled over. They always came in and if the dog was dirty they went mad, pointing at the mess, shouting and throwing the dog outside. If she was clean they would have patrolled first to check, then they were nice to her. They could not understand why this poor dog kept doing it. They thought she was embarrassed and guilty as her behaviour proved that she felt bad when they came in.

What an utter load of garbage this was. The poor dog was scared witless. I told them that she was so stressed she was more likely to mess, not less. To the dog, they left each day or night and she knew the next thing that would happen is that they would come down and go berserk for no reason other than they walked into the room.

They weren't entirely convinced so we set up a camera. Off they went, pretending to go out in the car to work. About 20 minutes later they returned. I did this on purpose as the husband tried to convince me the dog had poor control and simply couldn't wait more than a few hours and it was nothing to do with being scared.

They drove up, got out of the car, then back in and drove off. They never went into the house or saw the dog. The film clearly showed the poor dog shaking when she heard

- If a dog suddenly changes its toilet habits, get the vet to check it over. Urinary and bowel infections can cause problems for a dog just like they would for you.

- With puppies, take them out regularly, stand there and praise them when they get it right. Do NOT tell them off when they get it wrong or they will simply learn not to go in front of you, not that they shouldn't go in the house.

- If your dog starts to mess in front of you, clap or shout the dog's name to get it to stop and look at you then take it out. As SOON as it stops toileting, praise it all the way out. If you keep shouting once the dog has stopped and all the way into the garden, you will confuse and terrify the dog.

- No matter what you find when you come home, do NOT punish the dog. Once the mess is done it is forgotten about. Don't think your dog "feels guilty" because it is slinking around when you return. It isn't. It is terrified. You have taught your dog that coming in means you will be mad and the dog has no idea why and tries desperately to offer submissive gestures in the hope it will be OK. Do you really think your dog deserves to be terrified at the sound of your car or your key in the door? Always enter positively and be pleased to see your dog and clean up the mess quietly.

- Feed appropriately. You may have a breed or individual dog that is allergic to something you are feeding. Tinned food contains an average of 75 per cent water which has to come out again so don't feed it. Use a good quality dry complete food. Feed at the right time to fit your routine and the dog's age and breed. Ask your vet if you are not sure about this.

the car and running about frantically and wetting herself. They were made to do it again an hour later and the same thing happened. It was heartbreaking to watch this poor dog.

When shown the film, the woman started crying and the husband just sat there. I shouted at the pair of them that they should be ashamed.

I put them onto a simple routine. Changed the food to a dry complete, fed in the evening. They were told to start talking as they either came down the stairs or through the front door so she could hear their welcoming tone. They had to go into the kitchen as if they hadn't seen her for a year and make the biggest fuss they could.

Within three days they had a clean night from her for the first time. Within another two days she was clean all day and a neighbour was letting her out at lunchtime too. I got reports after three days, a week, a month and three months and she was never dirty again.

Running Away

OK, how many of you have dogs that run off but you are still letting them off the lead? I once retrained a dog four times because every time I had the dog recalling properly my clients were told to only exercise on a 50 feet training line for eight weeks but they kept letting him off.

"But he's so good on the line, a whole week went by and he didn't try to run once."

But in one week the behaviour wasn't modified or ingrained enough to become usual so within a day of having no line and therefore a different pattern of recall, he legged it. After four attempts I told them not to waste my time any longer.

Recall in classes is taught in a very strange way. Backed up against the village hall wall, you walk in front of the

- When you call the dog, sound like you actually want him, not like you want to punish him.

- Once the dog is on his way, keep calling. Don't stand there like a lemon. When the dog looks at you, you look like you now don't want him so he goes off and gets shouted at.

- When the dog reaches you, give him lots of praise. Put your hands on the dog's shoulders, press and say "Wait". Then give the dog a small push and say, "OK, go".

- You must always give permission for your dog to leave. Don't just take the lead off and let the dog run off as you are unclipping it. Use a command like "OK, go".

- Do it the same indoors and out until the dog is doing it all the time.

- If the dog runs off or is difficult to catch, be nice. When you eventually get the dog, be really pleased and praise the dog. Do NOT shout at him or you are punishing the catching, not the running and he isn't coming next time and neither would I.

- Do not let the dog off the lead until it is trained, no matter how quiet it is. Use a long training line in preference to an extending lead as the dog has more freedom and will behave more naturally.

- Some breeds are just not good off lead and you have to accept you can't do it. Siberian Huskies, Malamutes, Akitas, dogs with high prey drives and lots of individual dogs are not safe with very few exceptions. Of course, the huskies will just dig out if they can't climb . . .

dog, face him and call him to sit in front of you from about five feet or less. Just like in real life . . . NOT. This formal recall bears no resemblance to how we call our dog in real life so when you take your dog out, your recall is useless because you are not standing in a line or only five feet away and the dog isn't sitting facing you.

In real life the dog is usually moving and is going away from you. It may look at you briefly when you shout, but it is often not on the lead. So this is how you practise it: as you would for real.

Every time you shout your dog at home, that's a recall. If you shout him in from the garden or for his dinner, that's a recall. So do it as you would if you were outside. When owners shout their dog in from the garden they usually stand in the doorway, shout, wait to see the dog is on his way then go in. So how exactly is the dog supposed to know that calling him means come here, to me, wait when you get here and look at me? Either do it right all the time or don't bother. Until your dog is 100 per cent reliable, do it exactly the same all the time.

Neutering can play a part in this too. An entire dog or bitch can want to run off or escape to mate and girls can be just as determined as dogs. Dogs can scent bitches in season for miles so neuter your dog. Males are more likely to escape to fight and patrol territory if not neutered so go and do it.

Get proper fencing. It needs to be at least six feet high and have a section on top that tips into the garden that is about 18 inches wide and is fixed to the top of the fence. The idea is to have the top of the fence angled into the garden to make it very difficult to get over, like in animal enclosures at the zoo. If you have a digger you may have to sink it a few feet too. Don't leave your dog outside for long periods to get bored or wound up.

Pulling on the Lead

This is a common problem and often misunderstood. Owners often miss that a dog walking beside them calmly is a dog letting them lead. Note the *letting* them lead, not the owner forcing it.

A dog not pulling is showing you respect and has been taught properly not to pull. This means that a pulling dog often has other issues and hasn't been trained sufficiently. A dog that jumps all over you when you come in, eats your food and barks all the time isn't likely to walk nicely for you. So start by addressing your relationship.

Style is also another problem. Having handled dogs in competitive obedience, I am aware that the way I ask a dog to walk, with its head against my hip looking up at me in an arena bears no resemblance to how we go to the shops for a newspaper. If you have only tried to learn competitive heelwork, your dog may have no idea what you want when you simply go for a walk.

There are lots of long-standing "cures", such as turning and walking briskly away when the dog pulls, stopping, yanking the lead, etc. All of these are valid, but don't work for every dog, so be prepared for trial and error.

I use a lot of different head collars very successfully; again no one type suits all. I see many customers who bought one and gave up because the dog threw a tantrum, still pulled or got an initial result, thought the dog was trained and stopped using it.

If you use any kind of gadget such as a head collar or harness, use it consistently for several months or more. Once you feel you may not need it, try putting it on but only attaching your lead to the ordinary collar. See for about two weeks if the dog notices the difference in pull; if not, then you probably don't need it. Use the older techniques above too, don't rely on one option. But always address your overall relationship or boundaries or any improvements won't last.

Livestock Chasing

A farmer has the right to shoot a dog that is simply loose in a field with livestock. Remember that the term is "worrying" not chasing. The mere presence of a dog can be enough to alarm some animals which can cause abortion, heart failure and stampeding in which you can get hurt too.

Owners often misunderstand the chase behaviour and are doing things at home that they shouldn't be. Look at your overall obedience; don't just worry about chasing. You can't stop a dog chasing that doesn't listen to easier commands. Go back to classes if need be.

There is a piece of gun dog training equipment which is a canvas dummy on elastic which can have a rabbit skin tied to it. This is pegged out and sprung, looking very like a real running rabbit. It is a great way of testing chase behaviour as I've never managed to train a stunt rabbit! I do though suggest you only use it with a professional.

Distraction and reward with something the dog really wants is a training starting point. However, short of half a dead cow, some dogs do not find any sort of food or toy reward interesting enough. In those cases, the use of an interruption, such as an ultrasonic gadget can be the safest option, but again this is best done with professional coaching.

Sometimes a dog is determined to chase and the best you can hope for is control when you are with it, but never being able to trust it if it escaped. You therefore have to make sure that your dog can't escape. Rehoming has occasionally been the safest option, but most cases do at least come under control, even enough to be off lead as long as a human is present.

If you have a problem, consider these points too:

- Don't let your dog play with squeaky or furry toys which simply train the prey drive.

- Make sure you have excellent recall, even from other dogs and people or animals they know.

- If the noise the animal makes is a stimulus, download it from the internet and play it at increasing volume until your dog doesn't seem interested.

- The smell can help too. Ask a farmer for a cloth that smells of sheep or cows and give it to your dog. Familiarizing the dog to the smell and sounds makes the real thing less interesting.

- Do not follow the old wives' advice of putting your dog in with a stroppy ram or bull; it is likely your dog will be seriously or even fatally injured.

- A dog that persistently runs up and down and grabs at the fence dividing it from any sort of furry animal or poultry isn't playing and will kill them if it gets the chance.

- A dog that lives safely with cats and occasionally other animals is not automatically safe with every species.

Aggression

OK, here's the big one. You must read the chapters on *Relationship and Control, Buying a Dog* and *Play and Toys* as well as this section. Those chapters tell you how to avoid needing to read this section in the first place.

All aggression needs professional help but some trainers just can't solve it and would rather tell you to put the dog down than admit fear or defeat. Ask your vet to recommend someone, talk to other dog owners, do some research in the book stores. Once you find some to speak to, ask some questions.

• Have they trained your breed before?

• What methods do they think they will use?

• How successful have they been before? Can they talk you through some examples?

• Why do they think your dog does it?

• Can they refer you to clients whose dogs they have trained with similar problems?

The last point is always an interesting one. I once had an argument with a trainer at a class who said it was ridiculous to expect her to give new clients her old clients' details. I asked why. If she was as successful as she was claiming to be in front of a lot of people, why was that a problem? She got very agitated and said it was because of confidentiality. I pointed out I wasn't suggesting that she give details without permission but surely as money was involved it was appropriate for her to prove she knew what she was doing. She got very annoyed to the amusement of the people listening and said she didn't think it was right to be asked to do that and marched off.

About a month later I got a dog referred to me that had been assessed as a "put to sleep" case by another trainer . . . you've guessed it, it was her again. The dog was very alarming in its behaviour but it did not need putting down and I did retrain it. The original trainer had met the dog, looked terrified and pronounced it untrainable after about 15 minutes without doing anything with it.

I have lots of clients who will happily speak to new ones; some of them have written their stories for the website for all to see. Be suspicious of a trainer or behaviourist who claims a lot but can't back it up. I rarely see a dog with a problem that hasn't already been through several trainers.

Why do dogs bite humans or other animals? Lots of reasons: inappropriate play, the wrong toys, boredom and lack of stimulus, bad breeding, lack of training, stupid owners who encourage the wrong things and mental problems (dogs and owners).

Most dogs I see with aggression problems have at least two and sometimes more of the above things in their life. I have seen terriers that have ripped up cats and other dogs that also kill and strip their squeaky toys at home. I see big dogs played roughly with and encouraged to play tug of war that bite hands and arms. I meet idiots who encourage their dog to bark at and threaten other dogs and cats through the window and then cry crocodile tears when they kill a child's pet cat or dog.

How stupid do you have to be to not understand the link here? I am fed up with telling owners that tug of war and wrestling are not games. They are inviting a challenge from your dog that shouldn't happen if you are the boss. Don't flatter yourself that your dog gives up the toy when asked, he doesn't. Just don't do it – ever.

There is also no such thing as "play biting" or "mouthing". It is all biting and no dog should ever put its teeth on you in any circumstances. They use this behaviour to test each other. I have four dogs and they will sometimes do it to each other. What looks like a bit of play can

- Good obedience is a necessity. Go back to classes and get a good response to basic commands no matter how old your dog is. If classes won't have you, get a good behaviourist to help you.

- For better control, use some sort of head collar, correctly fitted.

- Stop all the stupid things you do at home.

- Stop letting the dog off the lead at all until the problem is sorted out. Don't take chances.

- Use a diet that is free from artificial additives, colours and preservatives in case your dog is sensitive to them.

- Don't allow your dog to stand on you, sit on you, ignore you, push you out of the way or challenge you. You have to have total respect from your dog or all the clever methods in the world will not stay put.

suddenly get more serious because one has nipped the other a bit too hard. It wasn't an accident. It was a deliberate test to see if they got told off or maybe could take over. So don't excuse any form of teeth on humans; it needs to stop.

You must get help to solve aggression. You may feel you know why your dog does it but you could be wrong. Everyone likes to think their dog has nervous aggression rather than just aggression; somehow they think that's a better version to have. It is dangerous to make suggestions without assessing dogs so this is just food for thought. Find a good behaviourist and get some help.

8

FUNNY STORIES

Why did I become a dog trainer? To help dogs of course! It is a very serious business with a lot of responsibility. You have to respect the fact that you need to be safe to give advice to people who have dogs with big teeth that might just use them. There is a funny side though. People's misunderstandings of what you said or just plain stupidity can be very funny. If sex rears its ugly head, there can be a lot of embarrassment and a good laugh. Mention castration and most men start cringing and crossing their legs and most women start laughing.

I use some hands-on exercises that I call "dominance exercises". They are based on how dogs communicate with each other which means lots of leaning, standing over and touching. I have found that over the years I have developed these, they have become a fast and easy way of reducing a dog's dominance over humans and gaining respect. After all, new dogs meeting for the first time make very fast decisions about who's who.

The problem with these exercises is that I try to mimic the "sniffing the back end" thing that dogs do to each other. Dogs that allow this from another dog are showing slightly less dominance than the other dog. Several owners have been bitten when trying to touch the back end of their own dog. This is not allowed. During these exercises dogs will try to sit down, spin away, growl, come up and nip you and even bark at you. The level of objection becomes a measure as to how much better the dog gradually gets against how disrespectful it is now.

Part of the exercise with male dogs involves actually cupping the testicles or the general area if the dog is castrated. As you can imagine, this causes both amusement and disbelief when I tell owners they have to do it. One older couple brought a very stroppy Weimaraner to see me. He was a very physical dog, pushy and nasty. They did spoil him a bit and he wasn't castrated despite obvious sexually motivated behaviour as the man thought he'd "become girly" if he was done. Utter rubbish.

We had the usual leg crossing conversation and I told the man how pathetically macho it was to object to something like this that would help and that if he didn't get it sorted the dog would continue with some of the behaviour. At this point we moved on to the exercises. This dog definitely needed his testicles felt!

I did the exercise first, explaining as I went. As I got to the testicle holding part, the man suddenly grinned largely and the woman cringed and started wringing her hands on her skirt. Having seen all this before, I was trying not to catch the eye of my assistant who was sitting with them as we often laughed helplessly at the reactions. I finished my demonstration and asked which one of them wanted to go first.

"You can," said the man to his wife, "you need the practice."

I admit I bit my lip very hard at that moment and she got up, very embarrassed. She took up position and she did try very hard to get her hand near them, but just couldn't do it.

"I'm sorry," she wailed, "I just can't stand touching them, they feel horrible."

We left that exercise and moved on to something else; sexual therapy isn't something I'm trained for.

Another male client once got very annoyed at being asked to do this, despite the remarkable changes in his dog's behaviour.

"For God's sake," he shouted, "I'm not *gay*."

Owners are wonderful!

One owner turned up with two dogs she had adopted from a rescue kennels. They were both collie cross types, feathery coats and one of them was a bit fat and the other was becoming very aggressive. At this point she had had them for about four months. The rescue they came from had not even neutered them and she said they were both males and had been doing a lot of mounting behaviour which the rescue told her was them establishing dominance, which was partially true. The smaller of them was quite possessive of the bigger one and got a bit stroppy if you went to pet him. The fat one was a bit pushy but basically both were nice dogs. I examined them both and started laughing.

"Well, there's a very simple explanation for this: the fat one is pregnant and the other one is the father."

She stared at me as if I was mad.

"Don't be ridiculous. They are both boys. I specifically wanted boys and anyway I have checked and they both have . . . you know . . . *things*."

I rolled the bitch over and pointed at her swollen vulva.

"This is not a penis," I announced proudly (I do have "O" level Biology). "This is a vulva and this dog is pregnant."

I checked to see if the owner was paying attention. She was looking the other way.

"Look, I am showing you."

"No," she said very deliberately "I did it with my eyes closed, I don't want to *see* the bits."

It is true that mounting behaviour is often used by dogs to establish dominance and has nothing to do with sex. Lots of owners have no idea though that it is for anything other than sexual reasons and this leads to some interesting conversations. A very well-spoken lady rang me about her two Cairn terriers, litter brothers about 12 months old. She wanted to know what sort of therapy I could offer. This was a slightly unusual word to use when asking for help, so I asked her for an explanation of what she meant.

"Well, I was thinking of some sort of psychiatry, you know, counselling."

I asked her if she meant for her or the dogs.

"No, the dogs. They have issues which they need help with."

"OK, what sort of issues do you mean?"

I could hear her almost forcing the words out with great reluctance.

"Erm . . . personal things . . . like erm . . . sexual confusion."

"I still need a description."

"They mate each other, you know like they are making puppies."

This last sentence was forced out at speed; she had plucked up all her courage to do it. I explained that they were at an age where they were competing to be top dog and that it wasn't sexual and that they often mount each other's heads. I heard a sigh of relief.

"Thank God they're not gay."

She put the phone down before I could admonish her and suggest counselling!

This sounds like all humour is sex related so I'd better tell you about some other things. Arriving at a house to collect a dog for training, I was amused to see the dog walking carefully around a large rug in the lounge. This was a huge house, expensively furnished and the family had more money than sense. The rug in the lounge probably cost as much as all the furniture in my house and someone had obviously told the dog that.

I asked them how they taught the dog to go around it, I was quite impressed. Their reply was that they had simply "nagged" the dog every time it tried to walk on it and he simply stopped doing it. Having tried this on my dogs I can assure you that it doesn't work and I still don't know the secret. Of course, it could be that my rugs are from Argos and the dogs know it.

People often buy dogs they have no idea about. I mentioned in another chapter about the lady who thought I was stupid for saying that her herding and nipping collie was just doing what sheepdogs do as she hadn't got it from a farm. The idea of breeding and natural instinct had passed her by. For some reason Labradors are also misunderstood frequently and are often referred to as ready made pets and not as gun dogs which they are.

Here is a typical conversation with a Labrador owner.

"Please help me. My Lab is driving me mad."

"OK, what is it doing?"

"It picks up everything, socks, shoes, towels. It constantly has something in its mouth."

"Well it would, it's a Retriever."

"No, it's a Labrador, you're not listening."

"No, it's a Retriever. That's what it was bred for, to retrieve things."

"Do you know what I mean? Not the long-haired one, the short-haired one?"

"The long-haired one is a Golden Retriever, yours is a Labrador *Retriever*."

This usually produces a long sigh and in my cross voice I make them go and get their pedigree which of course says Labrador Retriever. Then they sigh again and say:

"Oh no, I thought I was just buying a Labrador."

Running a rescue also brings lots of stupid people to my door. The point of a good rescue is to take unwanted dogs and find them loving permanent homes. As a good rescue I homecheck people, take dogs back if there is a problem at any time, neuter the dogs and microchip them. Of course, not all rescues do this and not all people want to rescue for the right reasons.

Getting a dog cheaply for breeding is a common conversation. One man tried to adopt a white German Shepherd Dog bitch from me. He already had a male GSD who wasn't neutered and initially he said he wanted her to breed with his lovely champion GSD. I asked about the dog's pedigree and he said he didn't have papers for him but he was obviously a champion. He got a lecture from me stating that if the dog didn't have papers he couldn't possibly be a champion and also it meant he had no health tests done. In any case no dogs are rehomed for breeding. So he offered twice and then three times the donation for the dog and I said no. About two days later he rang again except told a different story and gave a different name. I thought this was funny so went along with it. I said yes, he sounded like the ideal home for the dog and he could make an appointment. This he did eagerly and gave me an address and phone number. Then I said there was just one thing more. I needed to come to do a homecheck and meet his dog and speak to his vet. He put the phone down.

About two weeks later a woman rang and it was obvious

fairly quickly she was the same man's wife or girlfriend. Same conversation except this time she said they had been homechecked by another rescue that was willing to vouch for them so they could come and collect my dog. She gave me a mobile phone number and a man's name – except we already had his real name and phone number from the original conversation and the address from the second conversation although that wasn't the address the woman gave.

I left it until the next day when she rang again to see if we had followed it up. Of course, she knew we hadn't. I kept her talking whilst my assistant rang the number of the man from my mobile. Sure enough in the background we could hear a phone ringing and the man answered. My assistant had a chat to the guy, asking questions about the "homecheck" he had done. These people were so stupid. My assistant asked the man if he was doing a homecheck now. He seemed confused, said no and asked why.

"Because we are talking to the woman who wants the dog now and you are in the background, talking to me".

This produced a hissing conversation at the other end and both phones went dead. We never heard from them again.

You have to be very careful of people who want dogs for fighting. They don't necessarily look like or act like you might think and that is why homechecking and referencing are a must. Sadly bull breeds are often wanted by the people who shouldn't have them and rehoming them must be done diligently. It is surprising how word spreads when certain breeds are in your kennels.

We took on an English Bull Terrier bitch unwanted when a marriage broke up. She never featured on the website or on the rehoming list as sooner or later someone would want one for genuinely the right reasons. Such dogs also get stolen for fighting so we are very low key about these breeds.

At the time we had set opening hours and a small kennel block. One afternoon about a week after Daisy came in, a guy pulled up in the car park as we were looking out of the window. He was short, squat, covered in tattoos and jewellery and had a nervous looking woman with him. Yes it was stereotyping and not PC but one of the staff said:

"I bet I know which dog he'll want." We laughed but little did we know.

He came in to the reception area at the front of the building and was constantly looking round trying to see what was in the kennels. There were only 10 kennels and from where he was you couldn't see in all the runs. All the time I was speaking to him his wife looked at her shoes and he looked round. I just stopped speaking and about 15 seconds later he looked at me.

"Sorry?" he said looking puzzled.

"You're not listening to me, are you?"

"We just want a dog."

"Unless you tell me exactly what you are looking for you won't even be seeing any dogs."

He said he wanted a "biggish" dog, not a "girly" dog and so we walked down the kennels. He walked down the middle, his wife behind him looking in each kennel. He didn't look properly, just a glance. Daisy was right at the end of the kennels. Until he reached her he had been totally silent. Once he saw Daisy, he virtually leapt at the bars.

"This is the dog we want. We'll have this one," and he put his hand on the gate to open it. I jumped forward and pulled his hand off.

"No you won't. This isn't a shop. Come back to reception."

Reluctantly he came back and was very aggressive. I asked him if he knew what the breed was called and what their history was. No, he didn't. He called her a "Bulldog". I told him that she would only go to someone who had knowledge of the breed and could keep her safe. He said he knew all about them and stuck to this even when I pointed out he didn't even know the name of her breed. I told him that he would have to pass a homecheck to have any dog at all and this made him look a bit worried. He gave me a name and address and asked when I'd be going. So I said in the next few days and he got really mad, wanting an appointment. The whole point of homechecking is to see people as they are normally, not prepared, so I refused to give him an appointment.

Then I asked him for some identification. There was a strong possibility of him having a heart attack at this point as he went so red you'd think he had been abusing a sun bed. A huge row broke out, which was highly amusing as he had obviously given me false information. Usually it is a friend or relative's house, hence the need for an appointment. Enough was enough so I told him to leave or we'd get the police. Consequently, off they went amidst swearing and wheel spins in the car park.

The next priority was to move Daisy to somewhere safe as now there was a risk she'd be stolen. So Daisy was moved.

Next morning at opening time a couple arrived in a car. They sat in the car for a lengthy conversation before coming in. When they did so, they were polite and answered questions fairly readily until they were asked what sort of dog they were looking for.

"We love Bulldogs," said the woman "any sort of Bulldog really."

When I asked her how many "sorts" of Bulldogs there

were, she looked embarrassed. This was now quite suspicious – the use of "Bulldog" again and still not knowing the breed. There is only one breed called Bulldog. I said that sadly we had no Bulldogs of any description which made them exchange glances and they asked if they could look round.

I assume the public think people in kennels are stupid. To our total amusement, they made a show of going down the kennels, hardly glancing in them, making a badly disguised attempt to go straight to what had been Daisy's kennel. When she wasn't there they looked amazed. They started a whispered conversation about how could they ask about a dog that wasn't there if they'd never been before. They came back to reception.

"There isn't really anything we want today," said the woman brightly. (Yes, I told her we weren't a shop.) "Could you let us know if you get anything in we would like?"

The man wasn't happy and was desperate to know where Daisy was.

"My mate came and said you had a Bulldog here. Has it been sold?"

"You mean rehomed. We're not a shop. No, we have never had a Bulldog here."

Can you see a theme developing? So I played a trick on them. I got them talking about breeds and mentioned the English Bull Terrier and said we had had one recently and she was in foster care. Their eyes nearly popped out of their heads.

"Oh, that's perfect. Can we go and see her? Where is she?"

"Sorry, not until you've been homechecked."

This caused great consternation as they didn't want to give me their details. Suddenly it was a "friend" who wanted one, not them. I talked about the breed history and said that only true lovers of the breed with the right experience knew the breed and that they could whistle. Total garbage, of course, but I can lie beautifully if I have to.

I said they made a special sound by pursing their lips and that they did it when frightened. They said their friend would be in touch.

We only had to wait 24 hours for the conclusion of this story. Two men turned up the next day and were really quite scary. They claimed to live in the next village and wanted a family pet. They did the usual, chatted briefly, talked about Bulldogs and "those English Bulldogs" (OK still not right, but closer don't you think?). I said we had one dog in foster care that was being assessed but she could only go to an experienced home. Can you guess what they said?

"Not many people know the breed well," said the bigger guy confidently "When mine was scared, like fireworks night, she used to whistle."

It was the funniest thing ever. We laughed so hard I couldn't speak for several seconds.

"Whistle? They can't whistle, you've been had . . . "

They went, never to return.

I was giving advice in a pet store one day when a woman came in to ask about her two dogs. They were mother and son and neither was neutered. She had originally bought the mother when she was unwanted by the breeder after having a couple of litters and she got the son when he was about eight months old after he was returned to his breeder. I always thought this sort of conversation was an old wife's tale, but apparently not. She said the mother had put on weight since her last season and asked whether I thought it was hormonal. I said if you can call pregnancy hormonal, then yes! She stared at me with a look of disgust.

"Didn't you hear me?" she cried "They are *mother and son*. They wouldn't do that!"

I offered her my card and said I'd rescue the puppies when the time came.

Of course, there are lots of little funny things that happen all the time. I love it when people come to see the rescue dogs and confidently announce to their family and friends the names of breeds that are looking for homes that they can see and get them wrong. Or say the strangest things. A family with two children arrived one day to see a litter of rescued puppies. They got the usual lecture about why rescue exists and their commitment. They specifically wanted a bitch and not a dog. As they were looking I asked them why only a bitch.

"My children are eight and 12. They need to learn about reproduction so the dog can have a litter and they can go through it all with her."

I told her to buy a video and a couple of rabbits instead.

The lists that people come with when they want to adopt are amazing. They want a ready-made dog that likes dogs, cats and kids, is house trained, barks at the door, and is lead- and obedience-trained. It must travel in the car well, keep itself clean and know when to be quiet and go to sleep. Of course, the people with this list are not going to put any effort into producing this miracle dog. My answer is always the same:

"If that dog comes in here, I'm keeping it."

Years ago I helped in a rescue that specialized in puppies

from unwanted litters from miles around. One well-dressed couple who obviously had money turned up in a flashy car. The lady was at home all day and they wanted a puppy as a surprise gift for their daughter's tenth birthday. They had to have the puppy that day as it was the actual birthday. The owner of the kennels refused as they hadn't been homechecked. The lady started to cry and we arranged to do the check that day. They came back at about 4 pm to collect the puppy.

They chose which one they wanted, paid the donation, filled in the adoption forms, all seemed well. Luckily I was in the car park as they were coming out, bringing back a dog from exercise. In the back of their car was a beautifully wrapped box with a large bow. I had a quick chat as they opened the door, calmly took the lid off the box and put the puppy in, replacing the lid.

I grabbed the lid and dragged the puppy out.

"You bloody idiots, what are you doing?" I am nothing if not polite.

"The puppy is a gift. We told you that. We want our daughter to open the present."

They were deadly serious. They expected the puppy to travel to its new home in the pitch black confinement of a cardboard box and thought that was OK.

Puppy went back into the kennels with me. They were in hot pursuit and shouted at the owner. She told them they could hand over the box and they could take the puppy. I objected because they could easily go and get another box and paper and do it again. I suggested they put a stuffed dog in the box and I would deliver the puppy later. The argument went back into the car park and I took the box off them. The puppy had pooped in the box as it had been scared and as I picked up the box to dump it, it "slipped" and the poop fell on their car seat.

I shut the door and walked off. I know I am not going to heaven.

So there you have it, the trials of dog training and rescue. If it ever stopped being funny, I think I'd stop doing it. Thank goodness I don't think it will ever stop.

9

KIDS AND DOGS

It's no wonder in TV circles they say never work with animals and children. Both can be unpredictable, funny, maddening and loving. Dogs and kids can often have a very sweet, tolerant relationship but many dogs are totally freaked out by children.

Do not follow any advice here or anywhere else unless you are sure of your dog. Get professional help if you doubt any reactions from your dog.

We live in a world of endless tragedies where dogs hurt and even kill children. It can seem as if many dogs hate kids and I've been asked whether some dogs target kids deliberately. Is there a common factor in these attacks? Could dogs really hate children?

No, they don't hate kids and if there is a common denominator, it is a lazy owner who hasn't trained his dog properly. It is usually larger breeds, a history of bad behaviour and an owner who is too selfish to bother sorting the dog out regardless of the number of complaints received.

In some of the sad deaths of children due to dog attacks, the dog was known to the police previously and no action taken. You can't use these examples as an illustration of dogs hating kids. Dogs don't hate kids, but they can be afraid of and even intimidated by them.

Problems between dogs and young children can be created out of the best of intentions. It is important that your dog sees your child on the same level as you. This means that once you are happy you can groom, remove food from, walk safely, play with and command your dog, your kids should be doing it too.

The noise kids make is often a factor in bad reactions. Kids scream, run, cry and fall over, often all at once. This can seem strange and frightening to dogs rather than exciting and fun. It can help to cage your dog whilst it gets used to the weirdness of kids. Sit by the cage, talk calmly, but not in a silly baby voice or too high a pitch. Exude a feeling of confidence and calm, praising your dog. Give the dog a chew or treat or a favourite toy. Get the kids occasionally and calmly to approach the cage and drop in a treat.

If the kids have toys the dog is afraid of, it is NOT funny to allow them to chase the dog with it. Sooner or later the dog will panic and retaliate and your child will be bitten. Leave out anything the dog is scared of and allow it to investigate in its own time. This also applies to other stuff like vacuum cleaners.

If old enough, involve the children in training and encourage them to learn the commands and hand signals needed. Agility training is great for kids as well as dogs and the games described in the chapter about play are fun and interesting. Kids also need to be seen involved in feeding to show the dog they have the same rights over food that you have.

Younger children can struggle to give commands and to be taken seriously by dogs. Put a younger child in front of you, between your knees with you sitting. Put your child's hand in yours, with you both looking at the dog. If possible, get your child to give a *sit*, *paw* or *down* command. Otherwise say it with them, using their hand to give the appropriate hand signal. Put a treat in that hand and give it to the dog. This makes it look more like the child is doing it all.

Allow kids to explore the dog's bed and cage, holding the dog on a lead if need be. When finished, the child moves away and the dog is allowed to go and reclaim the space. This means the child is seen to have the same territorial rights as you.

Walking a dog is often best done by a child with the dog in a head collar for control. For smaller kids, a long lead that you hold and a shorter one for them means it looks like the child is doing more than they maybe are, but what is important is what the dog sees.

Where you have a large dog and smaller or nervous children, I use my backwards training technique. I developed this many years ago for a very difficult Boxer who had bitten badly. Whilst I could handle him, his owners were understandably afraid and the dog knew it. I had to devise a way of total control that didn't involve being physical with him.

The trick is timing. In its extreme form, the technique controls everything the dog does, so use sparingly. Generally I only use it for a few commands.

If the dog sits or lies down, you press the shoulders of the dog if near enough without getting up and say the command. If further away, give a clear hand signal and say it. You must see the dog doing it, not find it in that position and time it to match the dog just putting its weight down. Praise the dog.

You can control *sit*, *down*, *come*, *back*, *eat*, all sorts of things. Just get the timing and signal right.

Dogs are attracted to strange sounds and smells, so a new baby is an interesting, if noisy, toy that smells of yummy milk and has a rather interesting nappy to explore. If you know someone who has a baby, borrow dirty nappies and old, dirty baby clothes. Let your dog investigate all of that before your baby comes.

Screaming kids can set off prey drive, fear and interest. You can download sounds of children screaming and shouting and then simply play them randomly. It is sometimes a surprise to discover that your lovely dog hears a child's scream and runs barking at the CD player. Again, desensitize all of this before a real baby does it.

If you are setting up a nursery, don't keep the dog out. You'll be taking dog germs in all the time anyway, it's pointless to think otherwise. Let the dog have a good look at all the new things you bring home. The less interesting the baby room is, the better.

It is not a good idea to let your dog chase your kids round the garden whilst they run. I treat a lot of cases where the dog eventually grabbed the child, or the child fell and was bitten by the dog. Or, as in one case, the dog was seized by the police after doing it to a random child in a park.

Games, agility and tricks are the best way for kids and dogs to learn about each other. You need to think about how to help your child control the dog and gain respect, and for your dog to not be surprised by anything your child does.

I don't personally allow kids out with my dogs. There are too many thefts of dogs from kids, dogs lost because the child was happily listening to an iPod instead of watching the dog, or the dog is being treated badly, trained badly or taught bad behaviour because you couldn't see. Don't take the risk.

I believe that professional help is needed for a lot of dogs to learn to cope with children – ideally before the kids come, or immediately you see the slightest problem. A good behaviourist isn't going to write your dog off because it growled at or even bit your child. We try to help you; you have to ask.

10

LETTING DOGS GO

Owning pets and the love you receive and feel is one of life's joys. It is also a sad fact that pets touch our lives for such a short time and we often have to make the unbelievably hard decision to put our beloved pet to sleep. However much you know deep down it is the right decision, it never feels like it. Never punish yourself for doing the right thing, I am sure your pet never would.

You should look upon euthanasia as a gift. The ability to end an animal's suffering or stress is an amazing thing. It may be the last gift you give your dog and it is every bit as important as everything else you did in its life.

When is the right time? I wish I knew for certain, but nobody does. You have to know and feel it is time and not be selfish. Some owners do keep their pets alive too long. For self-centred reasons, they can't face life without the dog and so kid themselves into thinking the dog isn't so bad. Here are some examples of owners working through the decision:

I know someone who had a Rough Collie. This dog was 14 and had been a present from the lady's husband who had died two years earlier. The dog was the last link with him and she just couldn't face it. The poor dog was incontinent, could hardly stand and had to be supported just to change position in bed. He simply lay there, unable to do anything for himself and messing all over. This had apparently gone on for a couple of months this badly when I met her. I couldn't believe that someone who said she loved this dog could look at him all day like that. How could you say you loved him when he was so miserable and had no quality of life? I told her that if she didn't take him to the vet then I would and I said she obviously needed counselling herself as she had not dealt with her husband's death. After much crying and shouting she agreed and we took him to his dignified death. A few days later she rang me to apologize and said she was having grief counselling. The right thing but far too late.

Making the decision due to illness is an easier one than making it due to behaviour problems but people still use it for the wrong reasons. I got a call recently from someone who had adopted a failed police dog about two months earlier. Most dogs given to the police are a bit of a handful, so you know what to expect. The dog was hyperactive, destructive and didn't listen. Instead of training, they had bought a kennel and run and put the dog out in it. He ate his way out of that and trashed the garden. The man said they had "tried everything" and couldn't stand it any more and wanted the dog gone. I pointed out that they hadn't gone to training classes or consulted a behaviourist or tried chews and good toys or tried diet changes, so they were nowhere near having tried everything. He was unpleasant and said he had an appointment with the vet to put the dog down the next morning. I laughed and asked what sort of vet puts down dogs because their owners are too lazy to train them.

This dog was passed onto a rescue and I hope to God they never get another one. Don't think they were bluffing either. Any vet will tell you that people bring dogs in all the time to be put to sleep because they are too boisterous, untrained or chewing. Those are NOT reasons to kill a dog.

Compare that with the family I dealt with who had an extremely aggressive and deaf Dalmatian. The breed carries deafness but it can be tested for and when you buy one, you only buy from parents who have been BAER tested which means their hearing has been properly tested.

This poor dog had no chance. He was bought from a puppy farm dealer who told them that he had no mother of the litter because she had got out and run away. The puppy was bought from Kent but the breeder was a known puppy farm breeder in Wales. So the dog was probably inbred, never socialized and never really stood a chance. With such serious aggression (he would run across the room and attack you) and not being able to hear, there was nothing I could do. The poor family accepted they had bought badly and that this poor dog was highly stressed and unstable and therefore had no joy in his life. They were devastated and agreed he should be put to sleep. Totally the right decision but also totally heartbreaking. The dog was only 10 months old.

People often avoid making the right decision and take the most amazing chances. I went out to see a client with a young crossbreed of about 11 months. The owners were a young couple in their mid twenties and the lady was about five months pregnant. The dog had come as a young puppy from a rescue centre that had got him from gypsies. He got Parvo, a serious and often fatal disease, shortly after being homed. He was very ill and was in the vet's for a week on a drip but luckily survived. For a long time afterwards he was unwell and slowly made progress. The problem with that was the owners were so pleased to see him with some spark in his behaviour that they didn't realize they were letting him get away with murder.

By the time he was six months old he was a nightmare. Having never been socialized as a puppy he was terrible with dogs and now was attacking visitors. This progressed to him biting his owners over trivial things. The biting went from nipping to quite serious punctures and I wondered if he might be a bit brain damaged from illness and his bad start.

When I went to see him he just stood on the rug in front of the fire staring at me. Every time I looked at him he snarled. The wife was the only one at home when I first got there and she was quite obviously scared of the dog. She had a bandage on her arm and a plaster on her finger covering bites from him. We had a very long chat and I walked around, using gestures to test the dog's reactions. Basically he was totally unstable and dangerous. When her husband arrived I got a bigger shock. He had two bandages and numerous plasters on his hands and arms and apparently two on his leg also.

I couldn't believe these two had let this go so far and the dog was still alive. This poor dog was obviously not right and after more talk and testing I said how sorry I was after all they had done in nursing him and saving his life but that he needed to be put to sleep. They sobbed and I left.

About a month later I got a call from the original rescue saying a lady had rung them to say she had adopted a dog that had originally been from them and she wanted to keep it but had some problems. She asked if I would call her and help, I said I would. It was, of course, the same dog and they had sold it (for £30) to this lady who had two young children. The dog had bitten all three of them. Fortunately the worst bite was on the adult and not the kids. The dog was now living in a cage as they couldn't trust him. I was so stunned I was speechless for a moment. These utterly selfish morons had *sold* the dog to a woman with young kids. They told her they were selling him because of the pregnancy and that they couldn't cope with a dog and a baby. It was devastating to these poor new owners to hear the truth and then face having to destroy the dog. I so admired this lady; she was so upset and asked if I would go with her the next day to do it. I did, it was horrible, but she did the right thing.

How do you decide the time is right? One of my dogs had a wasting, debilitating disease when old and he gradually lost the use of his back legs. He was on treatment for some months but it gradually got worse. Every day I wondered if today was the day. I tortured myself looking for signs that he had given up. Every night I went to bed wondering if I should have done it. Eventually one day I could see the difference in his face. For the first time he didn't get up to greet me, I had to help him up and outside to toilet. I knew then he had had enough and didn't want to fight it any more. The previous day he was still pottering around the garden and even wagged his tail a little; today he was a shadow and wore a pleading expression. I am crying as I write this and it was five years ago. He was special in ways I can't describe and I will miss him until I die. I miss every one of them and I still think about them and how they died and I still wonder with some of them whether the timing was right. It doesn't occupy me as an obsession, but those are the biggest decisions of my life and I want to know I made the right ones. It gets easier to live with but it doesn't go away.

You know your own dog and you should be able to see when even if they can still get up, it has become too difficult. You weigh up each day at a time and decide if the balance is still in the dog's favour. Ask these questions:

- Is the dog still eating/drinking? If yes, how much of an effort is it?

- Can the dog still get up, maybe with a little help or does he have to lie there all day until someone helps him?

- Is he incontinent?

- Is he in pain or uncomfortable even with medication?

- Does he show an interest in the world around him?

- Would a medication change help at all?

- What does your vet think about the situation?

You sometimes have to evaluate the dog every day and decide which way the balance is tipped. You will torture yourself over it; we all do.

Illness

Sometimes these are the hardest decisions. When do you know your dog has had enough? Only you can know that. Truthfully we have all been in the position of almost hoping our dog would just collapse and make it known that now is the time. In reality this rarely happens and I have spent months with ill dogs just waiting for some miraculous sign that I should do it now.

Another issue though is whether to treat at all. Some treatment can be unpleasant and the temporary side effects can outweigh the length of extra life you and the dog get out of it. I know people who have treated elderly dogs with cancer with aggressive treatments and ended up with maybe a few weeks extra but had weeks if not months of unpleasantness to get it. The same dogs would have had the same length of time on increasing pain relief and not had the horrible bit in the middle.

Behaviour Problems

Whilst I have already said that stupid things like chewing and barking are not good enough reasons to kill dogs, some other issues might be. You have already read about the selfish young couple who homed their mad dog to bite another family rather than put him to sleep. You cannot pass on an aggressive dog just to avoid feeling bad yourself. Don't fool yourself into thinking that a change of environment is the solution. Trying to rehome a dog that bites your kids does not mean finding some sad lonely person to take it. Everybody has nieces, nephews, friends, neighbours, kids in the park, etc.

You got the dog so it is your responsibility to sort out the problems. If it can't be done, then you have to make the right decision. I see so many people trying to sell or rehome a dog that bites and often they don't even mention it. Your feelings are not the issue and never will be. Being too cowardly to make the right choice is not an excuse for passing on a dog that will hurt someone or another animal.

If you really have done everything, and I *mean* everything, then you have to face the truth. If you got the best help, got more than one opinion, asked the breeder or rescue centre for help, employed a good trainer and still nothing has worked and the dog is still aggressive, make the right choice. Don't do it if you have simply bought a few books, asked your friends or been too selfish or embarrassed to get professionals to advise you.

Aggression is not an automatic death sentence. Each dog and situation must be properly assessed by a professional to see if the dog can be cured or if the dog is in the wrong home. Sometimes it can be trained out of the dog, but you have to ask the right people for help.

Moving on

This is so hard it caught me by surprise the first time I had to face it. In my early twenties I had two dogs, an old collie cross called Patch and a younger Jack Russell Terrier called Sherry. Patch was my first dog and had grown with me and didn't have a bad bone in her body. These two taught me so much. Both bitches, Sherry had come later and they hated each other. At the time I was still learning my craft and it was hard work understanding the pecking order and how to establish it between two very evenly matched, same-sex dogs.

Old age caught up with Patch and she became ill. Despite treatment she died. I cried for a week. It was the first big pet loss for me and I was totally devastated by it. I couldn't work for two days.

I hated Sherry so much. Simply because she was still here and my first, favourite dog wasn't. It was so bad of me, but at the time I couldn't help it. I never hurt her, I just couldn't pet her or walk her as I couldn't cope with seeing that Patch wasn't there with us. This went on for about two months. Gradually I got better and poor Sherry got the attention she deserved.

I couldn't face another dog and at the time circumstances weren't right for one. A couple of years later Sherry had mammary cancer and was helped by surgery but it came back two years after that. She was an old lady by then and further surgery was a pointless risk as it was probably in other places by then. So she was managed on drugs until the time came when she was ill and unhappy and she was put to sleep.

I was just moving away at this time and the whole thing was too much. I just couldn't face more dogs. Despite working with them I could not believe that I could ever go through that loss again, it seemed too hard to bear. The thought of having another dog meant thinking about losing them and it felt like a real pain in my heart. Every time I thought about another dog, I felt so guilty. How could I get a dog and love it like I loved them? I was convinced it meant that I didn't love them at all, or that my love wasn't as strong as it seemed. I believed they were in heaven looking down and were devastated that I could move on to love another dog. In my heart I was letting them down.

It was two years before I got another dog, my beloved Sasha, mentioned in another chapter. I vowed when I got her that I would always have more than one dog and never ever be left with just one again. Even now I would find it much harder to get another dog if I had none rather than finding one when I still have at least one with me. It is difficult to say what happened to make me realize that I could get Sasha and it was OK. Time probably and the realization that my dogs were not sitting in heaven crying over my new dog. They are sitting there thinking how lovely it is that I love more dogs and that other dogs are benefiting from a special bond and home. They know one day we will all meet up again.

You must work through your grief at your own pace. Once when I lost my old Rough Collie a friend said to me that it must be easier for me to lose him as I had four other dogs so it wasn't as bad. I asked her if she lost one of her three kids would that be easier because she had two others. She was really annoyed and said that wasn't the same. In a big voice, right in her face I said *"It is for me."* We haven't spoken since. You may not understand how strongly people feel for their pets, but you must respect it.

Your next dog is **not** a replacement. You cannot replace pets, they are not shoes. Every dog is special in its own way and has an individual bond and personality. Even a dog of the same breed is still not the same dog. If you lose a dog and come to my rescue centre telling me yours has died and you are looking for a replacement I will throw you out.

One afternoon when we had a litter of crossbreed puppies to home, a lady and her friend arrived to view them. They were in their mid-fifties and one of them was visibly upset. They looked at the puppies in their pen and there was one little bitch puppy with a black smooth coat and a white paw and white chest. When the upset lady saw her she started shouting.

"That's her, that's the one. Is it a girl? I want that one."

I said yes it was a girl and asked why she wanted that one.

That morning she had put to sleep her old dog, a bitch that was the spitting image of this puppy. She had come out with a friend to find a dog as she couldn't stand the pain of being without her beloved Cassie. She got photos out to show me and was so excited she was almost jumping up and down.

"I can't believe it, I've found another Cassie. It's fate. This is my replacement for Cassie, this is definitely the one."

I tried to discuss the temperament of the puppy with her and was of course annoyed she said "replacement". She just wasn't listening so I made them come outside. I tried again to talk about the temperament and how this dog was totally different and it wasn't Cassie.

"It doesn't matter. I want that one, that's my new dog."

I asked her if she had any better reason for wanting her than the fact that she looked like the other dog. Of course, she hadn't and looked surprised that I had even asked. I asked her that if the dog had been male or if it had been a different colour with the same markings would she have wanted it. Of course she wouldn't. I told her she couldn't have it. There was no way I was going to give that poor puppy to someone who didn't want her. This lady did not want my puppy, she wanted a "Cassie fix". She wanted my puppy simply to make it seem as if Cassie wasn't gone – you don't get a dog for that reason.

She became quite hysterical and was shouting and insulting. My job is to protect the dogs and none of her behaviour made any difference. Whilst I had every sympathy for the pain of a lost pet, nothing made giving her that puppy the right thing to do.

At this point I lost my temper and told her to leave. I said that she needed to grieve over her lost pet and to find a dog she loved for itself, not because it was a look alike. She was nowhere near coming to terms with the loss and was simply trying to replace the dog and when this one didn't behave like Cassie she would be disappointed and want rid of it.

Her friend had to lead her away, still hysterical although I was close to it myself and was swearing profusely. Nobody has the right to criticize my professional decisions and insult me, however upset they are. No person is more important than a dog getting the right home.

About four days later they came back. In all fairness she did apologize and actually thanked me for not giving her the puppy. She said that she now realized it was for the best and she now felt she didn't want a dog that looked like Cassie as no dog could ever be Cassie. It would take time before she was ready for another dog.

There is no right time to move on, it just happens. The pain of loss is real and it seems impossible to imagine a new dog and giving your love again. Usually at some point you realize that your old dog will not hate you if you get a new friend. He will not be waiting in heaven to criticize you when you get there. Why deprive another dog of love and security or deprive yourself of the love and affection you can get back just because you know that for a brief moment you may have to face pain again? Isn't all the other time worth it for you and the dog?

Don't let people tell you that you are stupid because you grieve for a pet. It can be as real as losing a person and just as hard to get over. Get counselling if you need it, but don't bottle it up because you feel embarrassed to tell people about it. Move on when you are ready; it happens at different times for different people. Some owners can get a new dog quickly and, as sad as they are, they adjust in the right way. For some it takes a long time and that is right for them. Don't get the same breed, sex and colour unless you are certain this is a breed you love for itself, not because it is a re-creation of your lost dog.

I have never had the ashes of any of my pets. To me it is a reminder of death and I would rather celebrate their life. I would rather see a good photo than an urn. It does give some people pleasure and makes them feel still close to the pet; it just doesn't do it for me. When I lost my Rough Collie, Shane I wandered the town for hours, lost in my grief. I passed a shop that had dog statues and in the window was one that looked like Shane – not just because it was a rough collie, but because it had his face and markings. I bought it. Shane sits on my bookcase and is the only ornament I can't bear to wrap when we move. He goes in the car, pride of place. Sounds daft really, but when I look at it I see him as he was when alive, just sitting looking at me.

I have never buried a pet either. For a long time I have

moved about and rented and I just couldn't move and leave one behind so I live through my memories, pictures and my statue. My friend buried one of her dogs in her favourite spot, out in the country, a lovely idea.

All of you will experience the pain at some point. Don't let it stop you from experiencing again the joy of another pet or from giving your love to another deserving dog.

INDEX

Three ways to order *Right Way* books:

1. Visit www.constablerobinson.com and order through our website.

2. Telephone the TBS order line on **01206 255 800**.
   Order lines are open Monday – Friday, 8:30am–5:30pm.

3. Use this order form and send a cheque made payable to TBS Ltd or
   charge my ☐ Visa ☐ Mastercard ☐ Maestro (issue no. _____)

Card number:_____

Expiry date: _____ Last three digits on back of card:_____

Signature: _____

(your signature is essential when paying by credit or debit card)

No. of copies	Title	Price	Total
	Vegetable Growing Month by Month	£5.99	
	The Curry Secret	£5.99	
	For P&P add £2.75 for the first book, 60p for each additional book		
	Grand Total		£

Name: _____

Address:_____

_____ Postcode: _____

Daytime Tel. No./Email _____
(in case of query)

**Please return forms to Cash Sales/Direct Mail Dept.,
The Book Service, Colchester Road, Frating Green,
Colchester CO7 7DW.**

Enquiries to readers@constablerobinson.com.

Constable and Robinson Ltd (directly or via its agents)
may mail, email or phone you about promotions or products.

☐ Tick box if you do not want these from us ☐ or our subsidiaries.

www.constablerobinson.com/rightway